MW01656955

# MASTER'S

## GUIDE TO

# BASIC SELF-DEFENSE

# MASTER'S GUIDE TO BASIC SELF-DEFENSE

## Progressive Retraining of the Reflexive Response

MASTER HEI LONG

PALADIN PRESS
BOULDER, COLORADO

**Also by Master Hei Long**

Danger Zones: Defending Yourself against Surprise Attack

Dragons Touch: Weaknesses of the Human Anatomy

Iron Hand of the Dragon's Touch: Secrets of Breaking Power

Master's Death Touch: Unarmed Killing Techniques

Master's Guide to Basic Self-Defense:
Progressive Retraining of the Reflexive Response

21 Techniques of Silent Killing

*Master's Guide to Basic Self-Defense:*
*Progressive Retraining of the Reflexive Response*
by Master Hei Long


ISBN 0-87364-574-X
Printed in the United States of America

Published by Paladin Press, a division of
Paladin Enterprises, Inc., P.O. Box 1307,
Boulder, Colorado 80306, USA.
(303) 443-7250

Direct inquiries and/or orders to the above address.

# CONTENTS

# INTRODUCTION

It is unfortunate that most men fail to recognize the need for a knowledge of self-defense until they have been victimized by their inadequacies. It may seem that violence is so far from reality that fighting and self-defense are for the movies or "the other guy." In truth, the Bureau of Justice Statistics reports a disquieting and ever-increasing number of violent assaults each year among inner-city dwellers. Most of those cases remain unsolved by police.

A particular level of skill in the martial arts is not a tool by which a man can defend money and property from theft. Material things can be replaced, and they are of little value when compared to an individual's life or well-being. The term "self-defense" means just that: *self*-defense—to be able to defend one's body against injurious attacks. It is a human right to be free from harm, and a legal right to protect yourself from such harm. It is true that we pay the police and the courts to protect us, but in most cases, *protection* turns out to be little more than *retaliation*—after the fact. And though there may be some satisfaction in seeing an assailant punished, his discomfort will not undo our sufferings, nor will it lessen the humiliation that is incidental to being beaten up in public.

This book proposes to give the lay person a solid understanding of self-defense and a skill level that will allow him to prevent an aggressor from inflicting pain and injury. There is no magical solution, no deeply mysterious method by which you can touch an opponent in a specific area of his body and bring him to his knees. It is much more than that, and yet it is not beyond any man to reach a level of effectiveness that will benefit him both physically and psychologically. It requires motivation, a source of knowledge, and personal effort; the rest is a matter of time.

I favor the word *decision* in discussing the most basic requirement for accomplishing an effective level of skill. The individual must make a choice to spend two or three sessions per week in the effort. Whether or not one has the capacity to learn basic self-defense is not a question. Not all men have the capacity to become champions, but all men—and women for that matter—can reach a high degree of proficiency if they put forth the effort. Again, it is a decision that has to be made. The time to make that decision, that *commitment*, is now.

# 1 THE CORE OF DEFENSE

Many of the martial arts teach advanced techniques that rely on speed and anticipation–applying offensive maneuvers without the assistance of a prestrike block or slip to neutralize an incoming blow. For example, when an opponent draws back a wide roundhouse punch, the defending student takes a quick step forward, thrusting out a short straight-line punch and lands his blow before his opponent is able to deliver. The student's punch strikes first, takes its effect, and offsets the opponent's balance, thus neutralizing the attack. Another common technique is to throw a low side kick into the opponent's ribs or solar plexus as he advances with a punch. Again, the student's blow lands first because the length of the leg gives him a reach advantage over the offending strike. And again, the attack is neutralized.

Numerous comparable techniques are taught and practiced in the martial arts, and while these maneuvers are offensive in nature, they are used defensively. Whether a block-and-strike technique, a "beat-him-to-the-punch" technique, or any one of the many other defensive options is utilized, the core of defensive action is the basic principle that defensive motion must neutralize offensive motion. The student must elude any potentially harmful—or perhaps fatal—physical contact with the opponent. If it does not result in contact, an offensive motion initiated by an opponent cannot harm you: what doesn't hit you can't hurt you.

The main priorities then, in working toward an effective skill level in self-defense, are the movement of the opponent and the way the student responds to that movement. The student's response will determine whether a punch, kick, or any other offensive action will result in physical contact with the potential for injury.

Consider for a moment a new driver in heavy traffic. He is on a highway traveling in the inside lane. He is driving a brand new car, which he values greatly. Suddenly, a driver cuts in front of him from the outside lane, cutting across his path so closely that it looks like he will probably swipe the new car's fender. What might the new driver do, as compared to what an older, more experienced driver would do?

Without thinking, the new driver is likely to turn away from the invading vehicle, crossing the centerline that separates his lane from oncoming traffic, and causing a head-on collision. The experienced driver, on the other hand, would release his accelerator and apply his brakes lightly to avoid the offending automobile.

The options in such a situation are, of course, available to both the new driver and the experienced driver. The experienced one, however, will be more apt to take a rational course of action without panicking, and he would never consider crossing a dividing line into oncoming traffic. He is practiced in dealing with unexpected dangers on the road.

Because there is seldom time to think in such a situation, the actions initiated to avoid the most deadly consequences must be taken without premeditation. Every move the drivers make will be initiated involuntarily by the central nervous system, commanded by the cerebrum.

## The Reflex Arc

Reflexes allow our bodies to initiate actions that bypass conscious, deliberate thought in emergency situations. Sensory receptors in the peripheral nervous system are able to detect changes inside and outside the body. When such a change requires a bodily adjustment, the change will be made automatically. For example, when the body becomes very hot, sweating occurs to cool down the surface temperature. We cannot control sweat glands; they function involuntarily when needed. When sensory receptors detect a change that represents an immediate danger, a similar function is carried out by the nervous system. These reactions, called *reflex arcs*, are involuntary and immediate.

In the case of the driver, the reflex involves the eyes (sensory receptors) detecting the danger of the offending automobile. The information is then transmitted by afferent neurons through the central nervous system to the hypothalamus and into the cerebrum. The cerebrum searches the memory and makes a decision as to what course of action to take based on both the information it received from the sensory receptors and whatever information had been stored in the memory relating to the crisis. Once the decision is made, afferent neurons send commands for the appropriate response to the effector neurons of the necessary muscles, and the defensive action takes place involuntarily. The entire process, from sensory reception to reaction, takes place before the driver is aware of what he is doing.

Since both the new and the veteran driver have sensory and reflex capabilities, why would the experienced driver take the more rational course of action? The answer to this question is the beginning of an understanding of tactical self-defense as taught in the martial arts.

The key difference between the two drivers is the available information from which to choose a course of action. The experienced driver would regard a head-on collision as the most dangerous option, and one to be avoided at all costs. He might even turn his vehicle into the offending vehicle to avoid being pushed across the dividing line. The new driver, on the other hand, may not regard the possibility of a head-on collision as more detrimental than being hit by a vehicle crossing in front of his. His awareness of the dangers of crossing the dividing line may not have been learned as yet. (Once he crosses the line and is fed the new information regarding a greater danger, this choice may be deplored, but for the moment, the car crossing in front of him is the only danger of which he is aware.)

Again, the choices made in a reflex arc are based upon the information that has been detected by the reporting sensory organs or receptors and any comparable data that has been stored in the memory. Reflex arc or not, if the information needed to make a rational choice is not available to the cerebrum, it will be unable to choose the best possible option and issue the corresponding commands to prevent the danger. This is where we begin to understand the biological implications of training in self-defense.

## *Conditioned Reflex*

Consider two boxers in a ring. One has taken a hard blow to the head and is temporarily dazed from the impact. How is it that an experienced boxer often is able to avoid being hit with additional punches, even while dazed from a hard, solid punch? The capacity to think clearly and act rationally is inhibited by the influence of the heavy blow, yet a good fighter will still be able to duck and slip punches. The action involved here is called a *conditioned reflex*. Actually, professional fighters quite often duck and slip punches that come at them before they are able to focus on and make a voluntary decision to tactically avoid them. This is accomplished by the body's biological command center, the central nervous system, and, specifically, the conditioned reflex arc.

To further illustrate the efficiency of the conditioned reflex arc, consider the natural reaction to being burned. If you accidently touch a hot frying pan, your hand will jerk away from the pan before you have the opportunity to respond voluntarily. Clinical studies have shown that the hand actually pulls away from such stimuli *before* the pain is felt on the skin. The central nervous system, via the peripheral nervous system and the reflex arc, has received the information and has decided on and effected a course of action long before the conscious part of the brain is aware of the danger. Without the reflex arc, it would take a great deal longer to realize the danger and respond. Consequently, damage to the skin would be exceedingly worse.

Reflexes, therefore, are capable of responding to stimuli much more efficiently than voluntary reactions. This being a proven fact, conditioning the reflexes to respond to specific stimuli with specific reactions will make the conditioned reflex the most efficient—and the most effective—method of response in any self-defense situation.

The cerebrum can only issue commands with which it is familiar. Consequently, for the defender in an assault, as for the driver, a proper reflex response can only come as the result of conditioning the reflexes to respond in a desired manner. The conditioned reflex is the direct result of learning.

## *Conditioned Defense Response and the Conjunctival Reflex*

With exposure to the appropriate stimulus and by practicing the desired response, the student can and will reach a skill level wherein defensive maneuvers become second nature, bringing his movements to an efficiency level that will readily exceed the capacity of voluntary reactions. When the stimulus/response factors are integrated with a structured learning process, the conditioned defense response becomes a reflex arc (i.e., the conditioned defense response and the reflex arc have a reciprocal, or bilateral, effect under specified stimuli). This symmetry is our long-term goal in reflex development. The theories of stimulus, response, and the learning process will be discussed later in this chapter. But first, with a basic understanding of the reflex and its forced intervention, it is important to discuss the *conjunctival reflex.*

The conjunctival reflex is the one that forces us to close our eyes when the membrane lining, or the eyelid, is touched or threatened. The reaction is not only to close the eyes, but quite often to turn the eyes away from the offending stimulus by turning the face. For all practical purposes, this is an undesired reaction. Yet it is an instinct that will prevail over conscious thought *unless it is deconditioned.*

Such deconditioning is a time-consuming process; the conjunctival reflex works well with other cerebral reflexes that force the student to turn his eyes away from the shock and disorientation of painful contact to the face and head, especially if that contact is unexpected. But the instructor or student who does not consider the deconditioning of the conjunctival reflex to be a compulsory component of training is being less than realistic in his concept of self-defense.

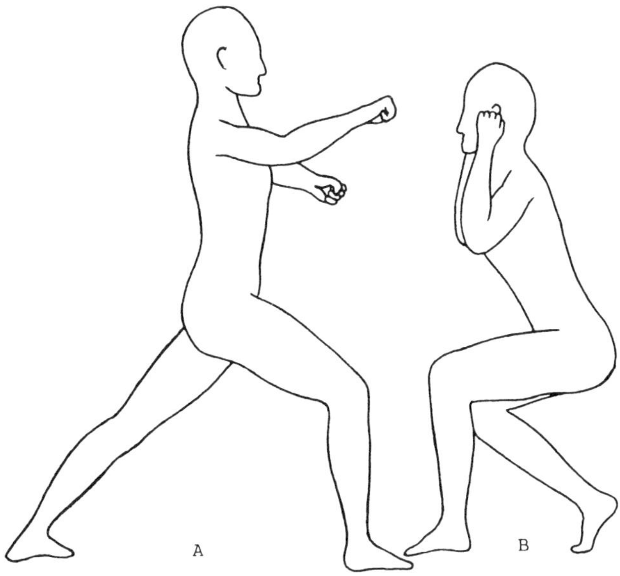


**Figure 1**

Observe Figures 1 and 2. The offender (A) has just struck the defender (B) with an unexpected punch, and is in the process of throwing a second strike. Which of the defenders is likely to be able to avoid being hit with the second blow? In Figure 1, the defender has moved his head from the position it was in when the first punch landed. The

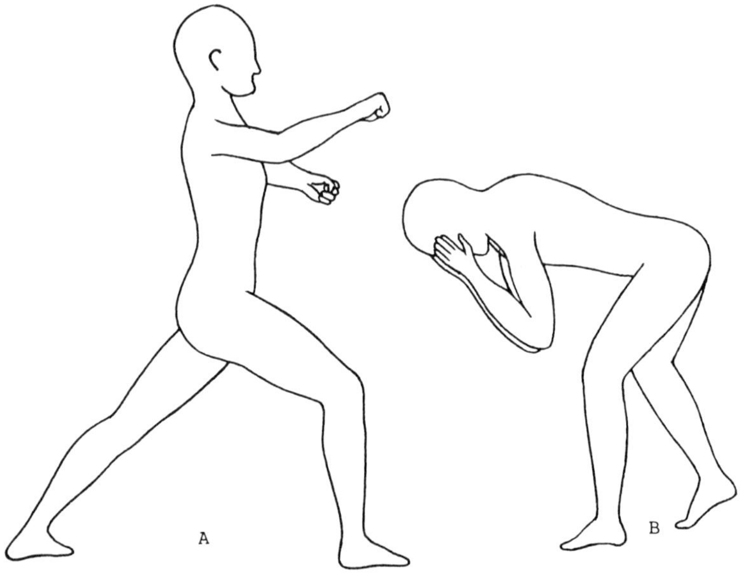


**Figure 2**

defender in Figure 2 has also moved his head from the original position. But their body positions are markedly different.

The defender in Figure 1 has ducked downward, brought his hands up close to his head, and is looking at the offender to see what he is doing. If he chooses, he can initiate his own counterattack from this position and be able to neutralize the second blow.

The defender in Figure 2 is a helpless target. He is completely out of position for initiating a counterattack, and certainly for defending himself against the second blow. He has not been trained to avoid the natural, instinctive reaction to being hit in the face (and especially in or near the eye), which is to turn the head away. The defender in Figure 2 could easily be hit with a kick, a rising knee strike, or any assortment of hand strikes. He will be unable to avoid any of these offensive maneuvers because he cannot see them coming and cannot react either voluntarily or by reflex.

A student might know a hundred techniques for blocking and counterstriking, but if he is hit in the face unexpectedly with a single blow, none of those techniques is going to be of any help in protecting him from a continued assault if the conjunctival reflex forces his head and eyes away. This involuntary reaction must be systematically suppressed and replaced with an alternative reaction, a *conditioned defense response.*

Within the science of technical fighting, the deconditioning of the conjunctival reflex—as well as other inept reactions to assaults—is the basis of the conditioned defense response. It is as much a learning process as was learning cursive penmanship—the replacing of one set of movements with another. Of course, the movements must be studied and understood, and a practical learning process must be gainfully applied.

## Learning Processes

There are four components of the method by which, hypothetically, all human beings—excluding those with biological or psychological pathologies—can be trained to develop a martial instinct that surpasses voluntary effort (i.e, the conditioned defense response). They are: exposition, instruction, repetition, and habituation.

### *Exposition*

Exposition consists of *exposing the body to the demand.* The demand, in the instance of self-defense, is to be subjected to various punches, kicks, grabs, and holds. The student must learn what these attacks look and feel like. He must learn to see them coming from his peripheral vision. He must learn to recognize the beginnings of such movements, and to anticipate them by observing the body positions of potential assailants. Theoretical studies are productive, and inanimate exercises such as studying charts and training on striking gear will be helpful. However, there is no substitute for the experience of blocking or avoiding a punch that was intended to make contact. The student must experience the speed and strength of offensive maneuvers, and he must also experience the impact of a blow. (It is not necessary that he be hit with full power punches from a naked hand, but the jolt and shock must be felt for a number of reasons, not the least of which is to experience the pain, and thereby learn not to fear it.)

## *Instruction*

Instruction consists of *teaching the body the proper responses*. Both the mind and the body must be taught how to respond to various attacks: when to block, when to avoid contact with the incoming blow altogether, when it is safe to use outside blocks, and when return strikes are called for.

Because of the numerous variables involved, instruction is the most difficult component of the learning process. The body must learn to execute new and unfamiliar movements, weight distribution and balance, and muscle control. The sources of such instruction include group or private lessons, text studies, and observation to name a few. But regardless of the origin of the information, this part of the learning process will be the most time-consuming and demanding and will require the greatest amount of concentration and effort.

## *Repetition*

Repetition consists of *familiarizing the body with the movements*. This stage of the process involves a certain degree of tedium. (As a boy, I was told that a technique practiced a thousand times is one that the student has only begun to learn.)

To reach a high level of proficiency in movement, repeated practice will be necessary. As the student continues the developmental practices, the techniques will become less and less demanding physically and mentally, and reflexes will begin taking over. In time, the movements will begin to flow almost without effort. Muscles and joints will move with synchronism and fluidity, allowing speed and accuracy to develop and grow. Increased training time at this point will enhance the skill level achieved in each session, eventually resulting in the development of the specified reflex arc, or the conditioned defense response.

## *Habituation*

Habituation consists of *the continuum of practice*. Developing the habit of biweekly training will keep the reflexes sharp and the muscles and joints familiar with the movements. Training must be as ingrained in the student's routine as basic hygiene. Once a particular skill level is reached, regular practice must be maintained to retain that level of achievement. The training of accomplished movement will be as much a pleasure as it is a disciplined effort, but it should not be taken for granted. It is much easier to lose physical skills than it is to achieve them. To adapt is a natural biological capability. The human body will adjust to demands placed upon it, and conversely, it will adjust to lack of demand by weakening and stiffening. To retain your level of achievement, you must practice as a habit. Reaching a high degree of proficiency and then losing it to laziness makes the entire effort a waste of time.

# 2 DEFENSIVE MOVEMENTS: SLIPPING

There are a number of methods by which a student can avoid being struck by an incoming offensive blow. In this chapter, we are going to study slips—defensive maneuvers that do not rely on the hands or other body parts to interfere with the course of the blow.

There are two major advantages to using slips as defensive maneuvers. The first is that the student is not required to occupy his hands in order to neutralize the strike. This leaves the hands free to counterpunch or initiate some other secondary action. The second advantage is that, when slipping, the student is not required to utilize strength against the incoming blow. He simply avoids the path of the weapon altogether, permitting the force to be expelled harmlessly. Allowing a blow to pass by in this manner places an additional tax on the offender because he must utilize strength and energy to bring the weapon back under control and return it to the point of origin before using it again. Quite often, the free-moving weapon will pull him off balance as well.

Slipping is a very important element in the structure of the defensive system being taught in this text. A program for bringing the movements to a high level of efficiency will be discussed in later chapters. For the moment, study the details of these movements carefully and familiarize yourself with the variations.

## Parallel Slip

In Figure 3, you are standing with your left foot in front of your right. The toe of your right foot should be about six inches behind the heel of your left. The width of the stance should be close to the span of your shoulders, just inside or outside the spread of the shoulder caps. While the length and width of the stance must be determined by the comfort of the student and his individual proportions, the stance should not drift too far from these basic guidelines.

The body weight is distributed evenly on the legs, with the heel of the rear foot off the floor. The knees are bent slightly, and the stance is characterized by a readiness to spring quickly forward or backward. For this exercise, we will be concentrating on movements that do not include the use of the hands, so they should be behind the back and out of the way. Note the perpendicular lines that cross in the center of the face in Figure 3. These will show the extent of the movement being studied.

Figure 4 shows a right-side parallel slip. The position of the feet has not changed, but the hips and upper body have tilted to the right side, removing the head from the target area. Eyes, face, and head are kept in a forward position, with the eyes fixed on the offender. This is a very basic—but very effective—defensive movement.

Observe Figure 5. Your starting position is the same;

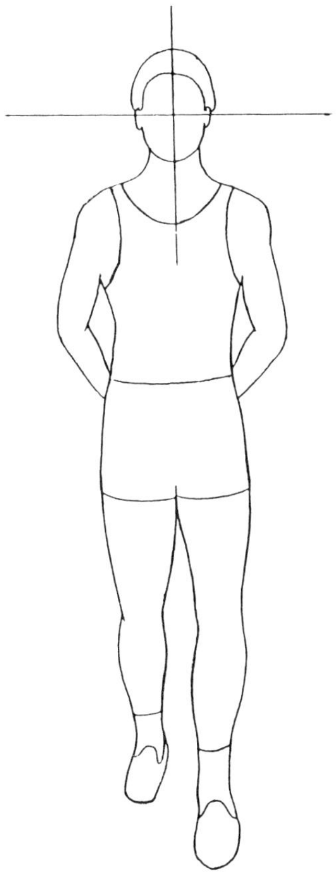

**Figure 3**

**Figure 4**

we will be working the entire system from this one position, so it will be a constant factor throughout the text. Basically, you have done the same thing in Figure 6 that you did in Figure 4, but to the opposite side. Here, you have tilted to the left at the hips and shoulders. The goal is the same: to remove the head from the target area.

When practicing parallel slips, be aware of your balance and any shift of body weight that is required to maintain a stable foundation through the legs and feet. You do not want to come up on the toes or heels beyond the formula of the stance (right heel raised slightly).

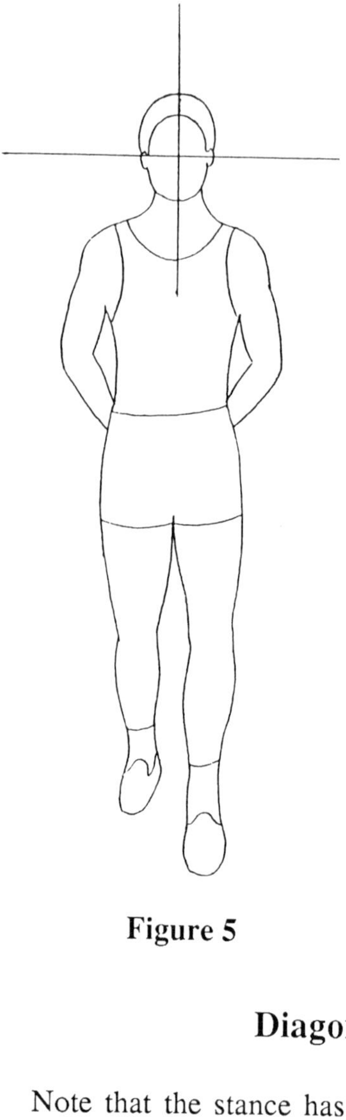

**Figure 5**

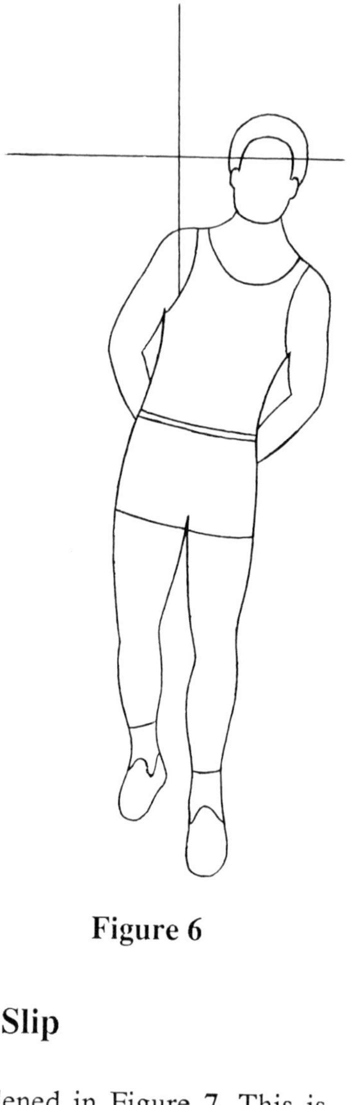

**Figure 6**

## Diagonal Slip

Note that the stance has widened in Figure 7. This is because the extent of the movement that will be used calls for a wider base. Observe Figure 8. You have again slipped to the right, but you have also dropped the head downward by approximately two feet. This kind of slip, a right-side diagonal slip, is best suited to defend against a wide roundhouse or wide overhand type of punch when you are

**Figure 7**

**Figure 8**

**Figure 9**

unsure of precisely where the punch will land. To achieve the movement, you must tilt the upper body to the side and slightly forward while bending the knees.

Figure 9 depicts a "finish" position. You do not want to rest in the previous, downward position because of the limitations it imposes on secondary movements. After using this slip, it is important to return immediately to the starting position or some other secondary position.

Observe Figures 10 through 12. Here again, you have accomplished a diagonal slip as in the previous sequence, but this time to the left side of the body. You will want to use the left diagonal slip against an offensive right hand,

Figure 10

Figure 11

Figure 12

and the right diagonal slip against an offensive left hand. These deep movements can also be applied when defending against small, hand-held weapons.

## Forward Slip

Recall the discussion on instinct and reflex in chapter 1, and the two illustrations that depicted the varied responses to an attack to the face (Figures 1 and 2). The most critical element of the forward slip, illustrated in Figures 13 through 15, is keeping the head tilted back and the eyes forward and focused on the opponent.

**Figure 13**

**Figure 14**

**Figure 15**

You have tilted the upper body slightly forward by bending at the waist and knees and dropped your head downward twenty to thirty inches. As with all deep slips, you must return to the starting position (Figure 15) immediately following the movement. Again, be aware of balance as you practice these movements, and make any necessary adjustments to the stance to maintain a solid foundation.

## Slip and Weave

The next five illustrations depict a classic defensive maneuver that is used in nearly every martial art—the slip and weave. The head will make an oval movement from point of origin to point of completion, constantly traveling away from the offensive stroke. This movement is designed for avoiding heavy weapons aimed at the head (e.g., a baseball bat or similarly long and heavy object). It is also useful against long, sharp cutting instruments, such as swords or machetes. In combat against skilled opponents, the slip and weave is especially effective against long, superpowered kicks, such as the 360-degree crescent kick or the 360-degree hook kick, wherein the stroke of the movement is so powerful that contacting the leg to block it often results in damage to the blocking arm and/or knocks the defender off balance.

Figures 16 through 18 depict the first half of the arc. Note the tilt of the body in 17, as opposed to the centered position in 18. As the arc reaches midpoint (Figure 18), the upper half of the torso is centered over the legs. The knees are bent most deeply at this point. Take special notice of the position of the head. The defender here is looking up and at his opponent. He has achieved sufficient clearance from the stroke of a head shot without tilting his head and eyes downward.

In this slip and weave, the defender fades down and to the right in his initial movement in order to defend against a stroke to the left side of the head. When the defender is poised in the position shown in Figure 18, the offending weapon should be passing almost directly over his head, clearing it by about twenty-five inches.

In Figure 19, the defender is coming out of the deepest point of the weave and is ascending in another arc to complete the oval. He is now tilted to the left. In Figure 20, the movement is completed and the defender is back in the starting position. This movement should also be practiced

Figure 16

Figure 17

Figure 18

Figure 19

Figure 20

in reverse, beginning the oval by leaning to the left side and coming out on the right.

## Step and Slide

The step and slide is designed to defend against lunging attacks directed at the centerline of the body (the centerline is shown in Figure 21). An example of such an attack would be a knife thrust to the stomach or face, or a jabbing strike with a pole or similar weapon.

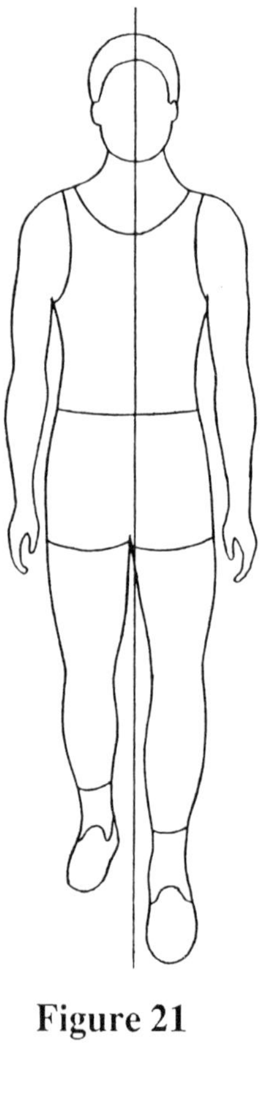

**Figure 21**

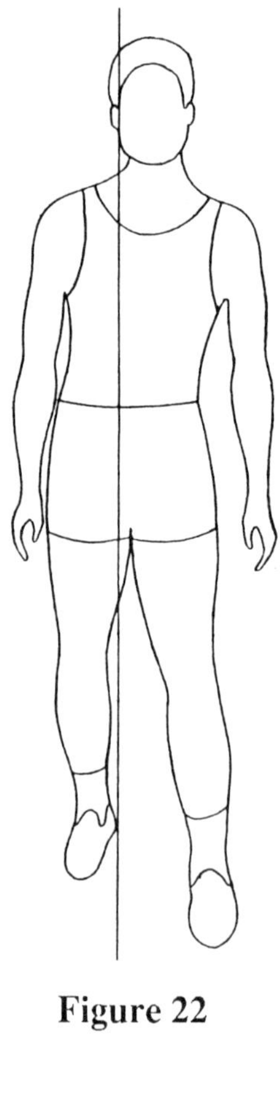

**Figure 22**

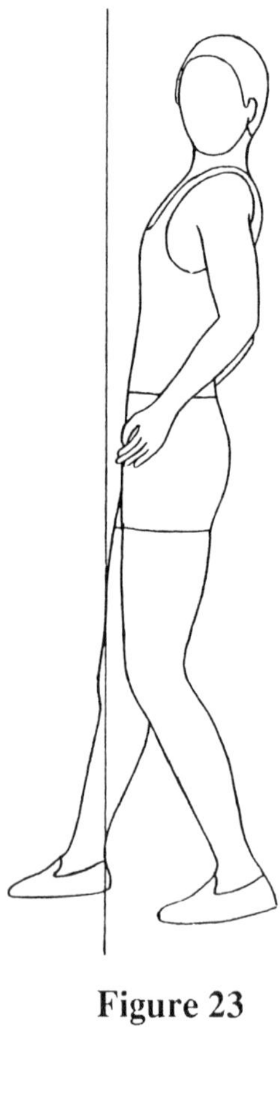

**Figure 23**

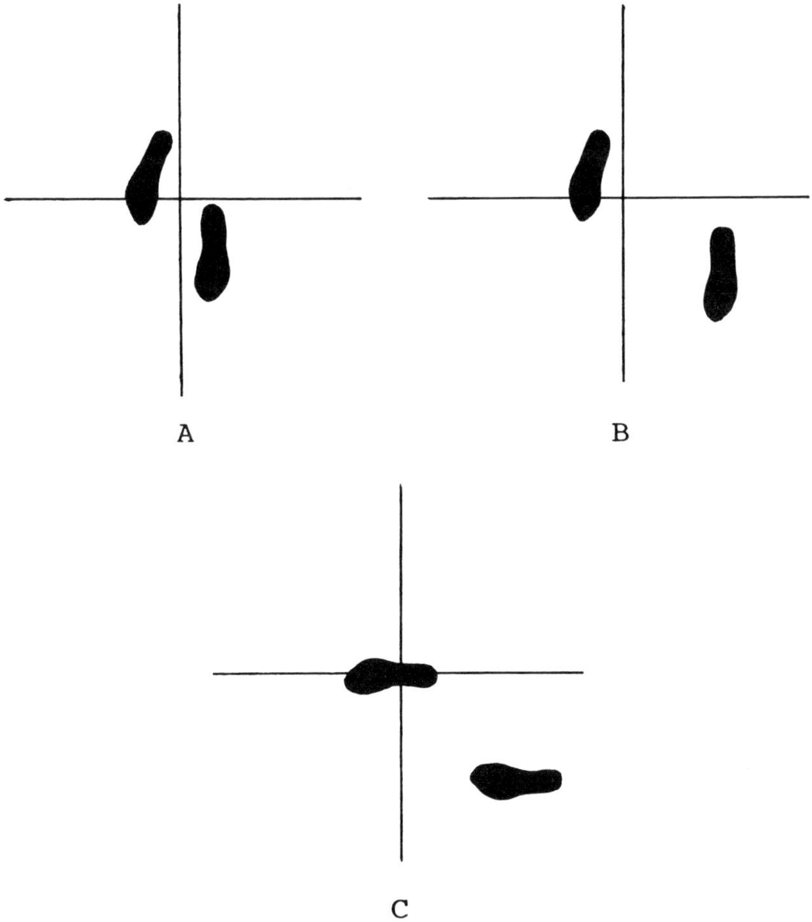


**Figure 24**

In Figure 22, the lead foot has moved slightly to the outside, and the upper body has tilted in the same direction. Figure 23 depicts the completed movement. Note that the feet have rotated to the right, but the right foot did not leave the ground—it only pivots. The left leg is bent, while the right leg is straight, and the upper half of the body is

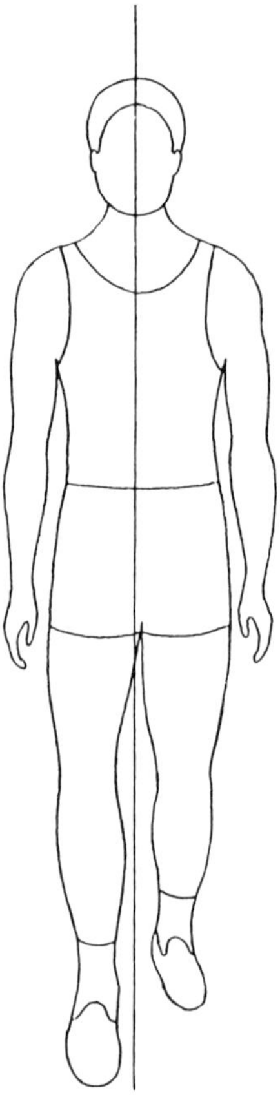

Figure 25

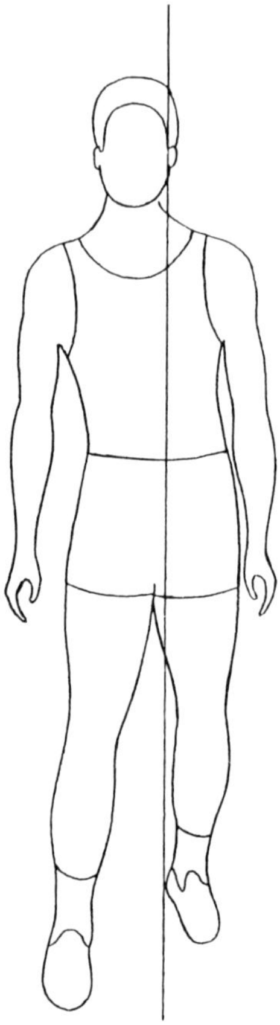

Figure 26

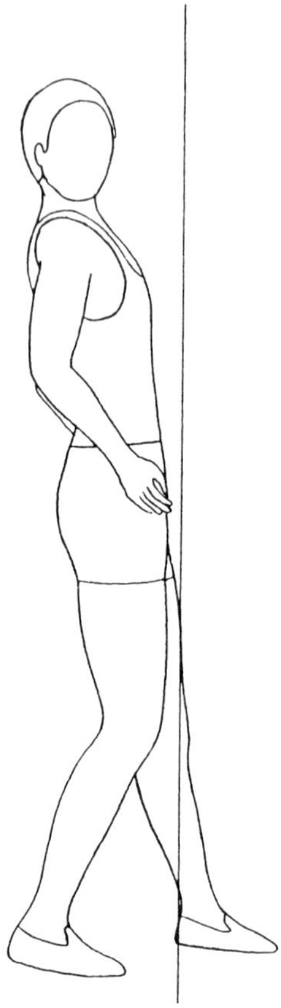

Figure 27

leaning back slightly. The initial step, the rotation of the feet, and the lean are all performed in continuous sequence, almost simultaneously, for a smooth, flowing motion. Looking at the location of the target line in Figure 21 and then in Figure 23, you will see that with just a short step and a pivot, the majority of the body has been removed from the target line altogether. Figure 24 shows your starting stance (A), your first step (B), and the pivot of the feet (C). Figures 25 through 27 illustrate the same movement, but starting with the left foot in back for comparison.

# 3 DEFENSIVE MOVEMENTS: FORMULA BLOCKING

When you have become familiar with the slipping movements in chapter 2, you will be ready to add some basic formula blocks to your defensive system. The term "formula" is used because each set of blocks used in Lian Shi follows a specific, progressive pattern. They begin with the set covered in this chapter, and each successive set requires a particular skill level achieved through experience with and understanding of the movements taught at the lower level.

## The Defensive Gates

At this stage of learning, the student will be training with four areas of proximity to his body, called *gates*. The purpose of the gates is to divide these proximities and, in effect, assign a hand and a block to each area for defensive purposes. Of course, the gates and the assigned blocking techniques expand as the system advances, but to avoid frustrating and confusing the beginning student, we will

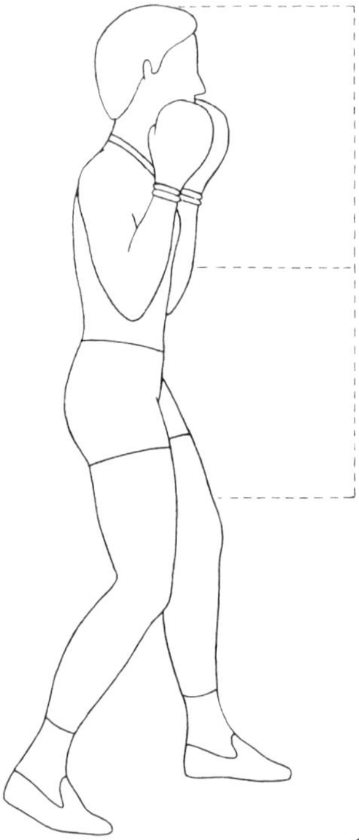

**Figure 28**

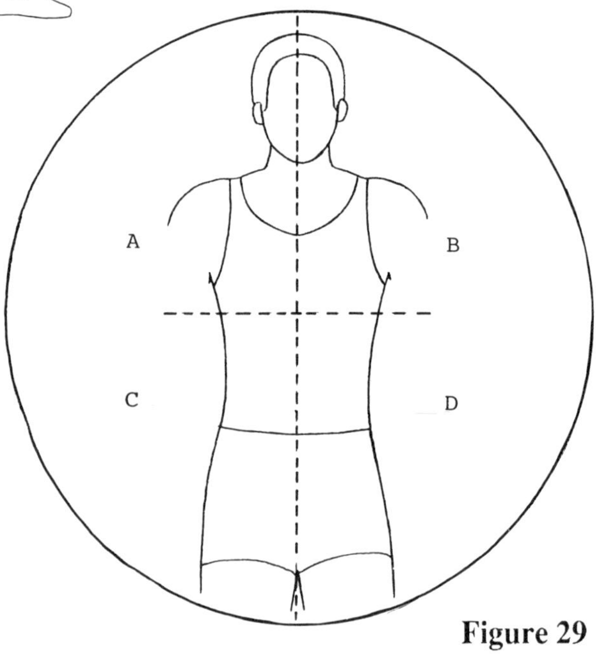


**Figure 29**

start by working with four gates and four blocks to defend them. Coupled with the slips taught in chapter 2, these four blocks form a solid defensive system with which to pursue an effective practice of self-defense.

Observe Figure 28. Note first that the position of the lower body is the same one that was taught for slips. We have added the hands now, and we will be working from this basic position from here on out.

We use this simplified position for two reasons. First, it is most natural one to assume from a normal walking or standing position, and second, the hands are held high and close to the body, which protects the jawline and ribs, two commonly injured areas in personal combat. Note that the left hand and shoulder are held slightly more forward than the right, giving the upper body a horizontal tilt. This brings the left hand closer to the opponent for quick, short jabs and will give the right hand extra motion from the hip and shoulder for delivering power punches.

Notice the dotted lines that cross in front of the body in Figure 29. These divide the four gates: upper right, upper left, lower right, and lower left. The crossing palm block is used to defend the upper gates, where the rule is that any stroke entering the upper left gate (B) will be blocked by the right hand, and a stroke entering the upper right gate (A) will be blocked by the left hand. A blow entering the upper half along the dividing line may be blocked by either hand.

For the lower gates, we will be using the 180-degree vertical palm block. The rule here is that any stroke entering the lower left gate (D) will be blocked by the left hand, and any stroke entering the lower right gate (C) will be blocked by the right hand. You would not want to reach into the lower right gate and bring an incoming blow to the outside of the left gate, because you would be carrying the blow farther than necessary to neutralize it.

## *Crossing Palm Block*

Figure 30 is a head-on view of the upper body, with the upper right and upper left gates sectioned off by a straight dotted line down the center.

Look at the original position of the left hand, shown by the dotted line. This is the ready position. The black oval just to the right of the dividing line shows where the object entered the perimeter of the defensive gate. Observe the course of the left hand executing a crossing palm block. The object is met by the palm at its point of entry into the perimeter of the right upper gate and is deflected from the face.

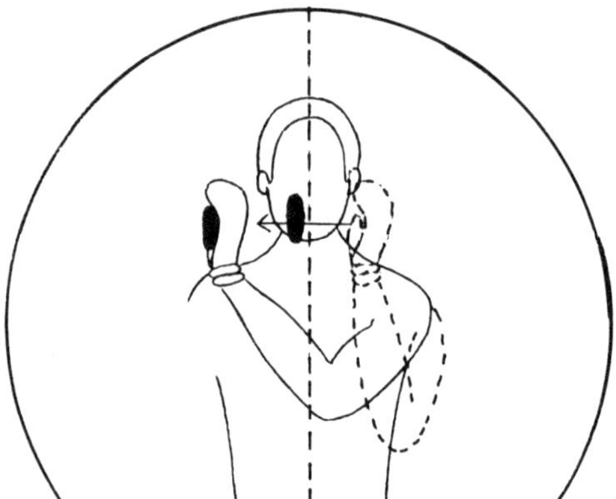

**Figure 30**

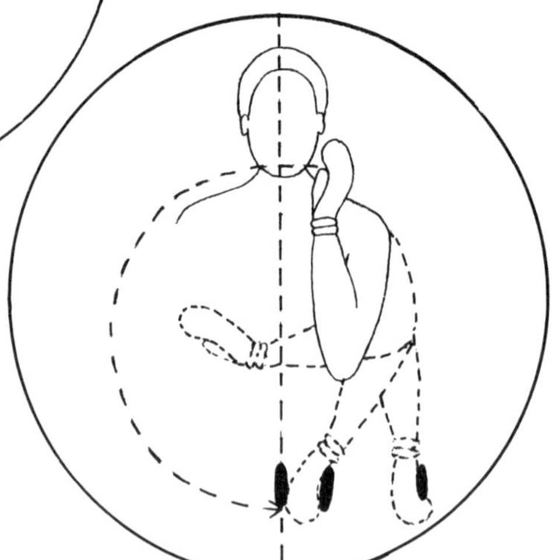

**Figure 31**

### *180-Degree Vertical Palm Block*

Observe Figure 31. This is another head-on view of the upper body, with the upper right and upper left gates sectioned off by a straight dotted line down the center. The stroke's point of origin is depicted with solid black lines, the path and the completion point in dotted lines.

The black oval resting on the centerline entered the perimeter of the lower gate dead center. The palm of the left hand meets it with a vertical palm block and carries it outside the span of the hip. Notice that the palm is turned to the outside of the body and the hand is pointed downward, as opposed to the position of the hand in the crossing palm block used for the upper gates.

## Blocking Applied

In the next eight illustrations, you will observe a side view of the crossing and vertical palm blocks. Take special note of how far the hands reach out to meet the object.

In Figure 32, the object is coming toward the upper gates. In Figure 33, the left hand reaches out to catch it in the palm and carry it to the outside of the opposite gate. Since the left hand was used to execute the crossing palm block, which gate did the object penetrate, the upper right or the upper left? Keep the rules for cross blocking in mind: the left hand guards the right upper gate, the right hand guards the left upper gate. An object entering along the centerline of the gates—both upper and lower—may be blocked by either corresponding hand. In this case, the object penetrated the upper right gate.

Look now at Figure 34. Note the extension of the blocking hand (solid lines). The dotted-line hand and arm depict the original position and thus the limit of the arm's extension in reaching for the block. When blocking, the

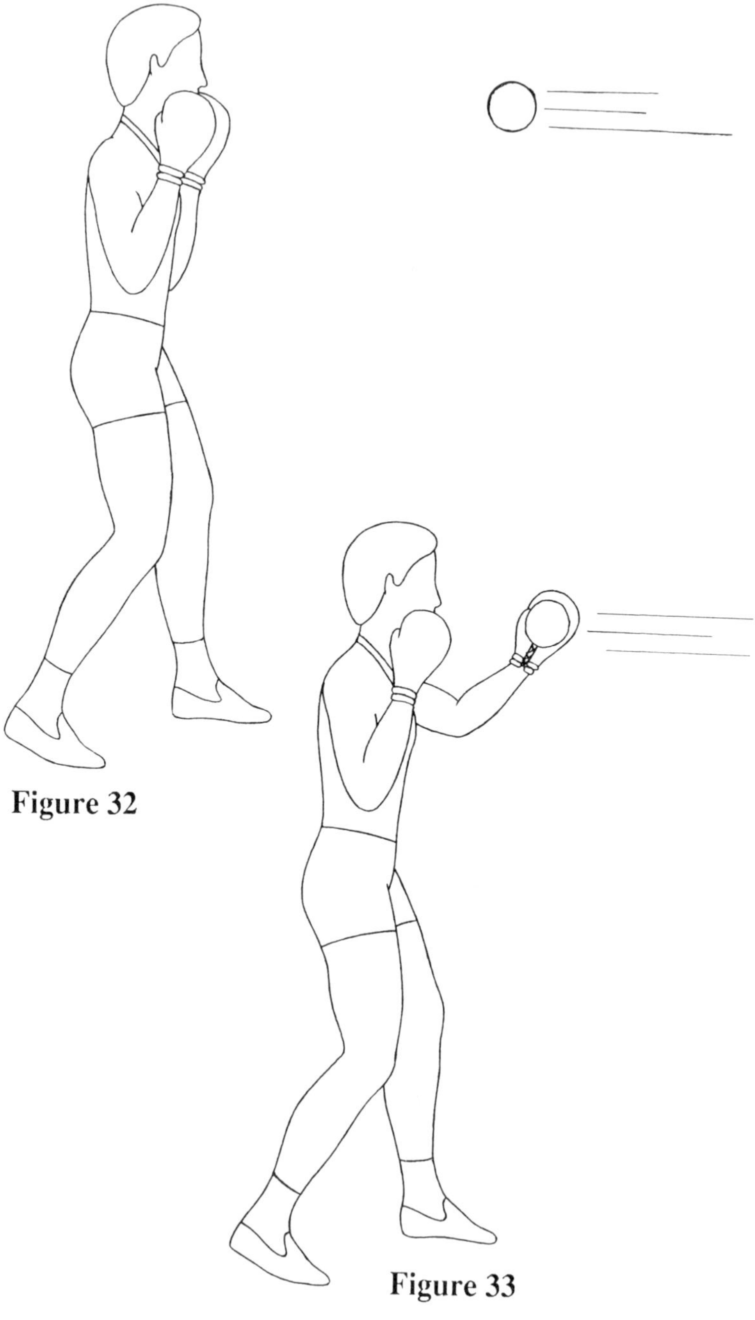

Figure 32

Figure 33

Figure 34

Figure 35

**Figure 36**

further the arm travels from the body, the weaker the block. Keep your blocks a maximum distance of eighteen to twenty inches from your body.

Again there is an object advancing toward the upper gates in Figure 35. In Figure 36, the right hand has reached out to block. Through which gate did the object penetrate?

In Figure 37, an object is advancing toward the lower gates. In Figure 38, the left hand has dropped forward in preparation for a vertical palm block. Note that the hand has rotated to the palm-down position by this point. In Figure 39, the arc is completed and the block has carried

**Figure 37**

**Figure 38**

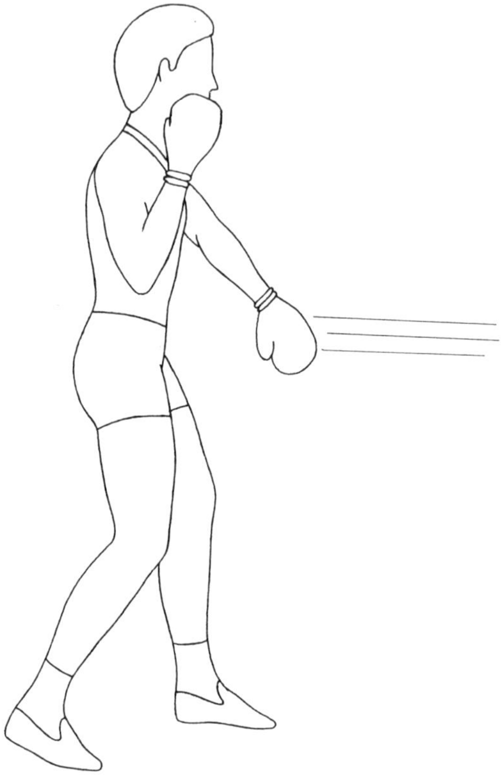

**Figure 39**

the object to the outside of the left hip. Note that the thumb is now facing the body and the palm is rotated to the outside of the body.

# 4 TOOLS FOR RETRAINING REFLEXES

One of the ingredients of effective and successful training is safety. There will always be some degree of risk involved in martial arts training, but through the use of tools and technology, the risks—especially at the early stages—may be substantially diminished. This chapter will introduce the reader to some of the tools which will not only promote safe practice sessions, but actually increase the level of effectiveness of those sessions.

Pay close attention to the details and descriptions of these tools, as they will be integrated into the training processes addressed in the next chapter.

## The Pugil Stick

Start with a six-foot-long wooden stick that is approximately one inch in diameter, as seen in Figure 40. (These are sold in hardware stores, building-supply houses, and comparable retail establishments.)

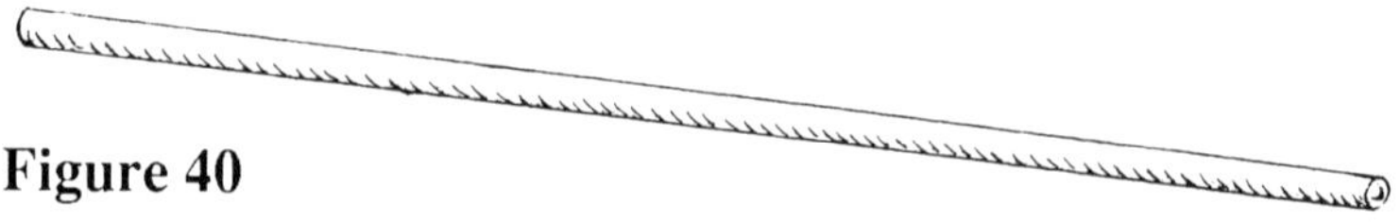

Figure 40

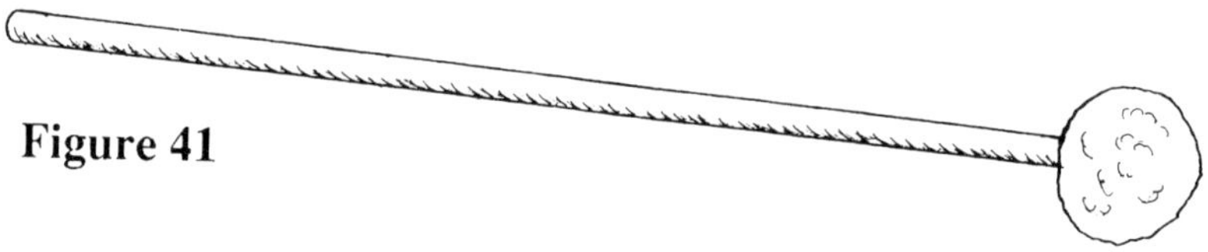

Figure 41

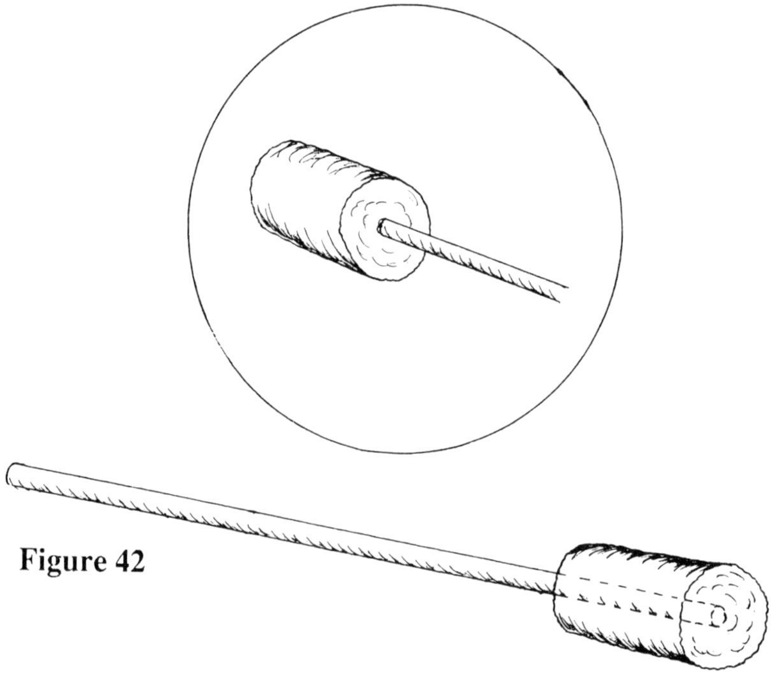

Figure 42

Next, you'll need a ball of tightly compressed cotton, as seen in Figure 41. You will find it in stores that sell upholstery supplies. Use a small amount of quick-drying glue to hold it to the tip of the stick. Wrap a piece of cloth around it to hold it in place. Use a piece of tape to hold the cloth to the stick. As in Figure 42, wrap an additional length of cotton, approximately eighteen inches in width, around the stick. The cotton wrap should extend about six inches from the circumference of the stick. A quick-drying glue should again be used to help hold the cotton in place.

Figure 43

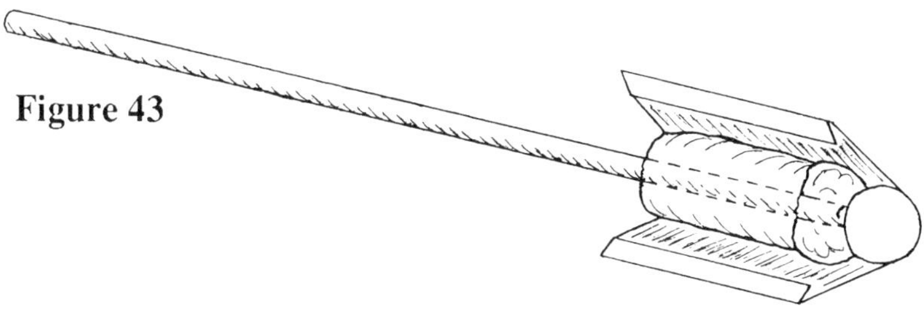

Figure 44

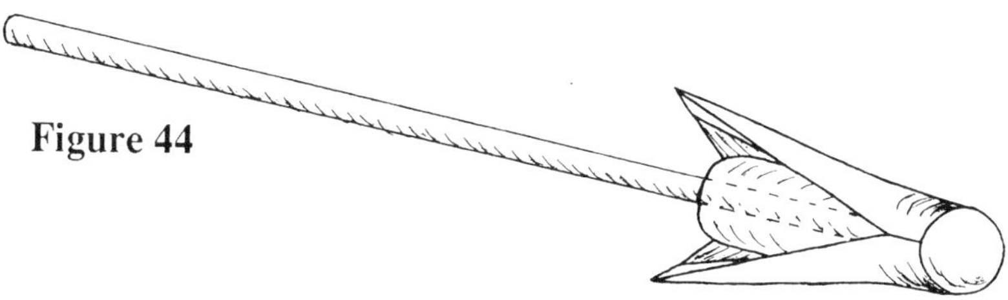

Figure 45

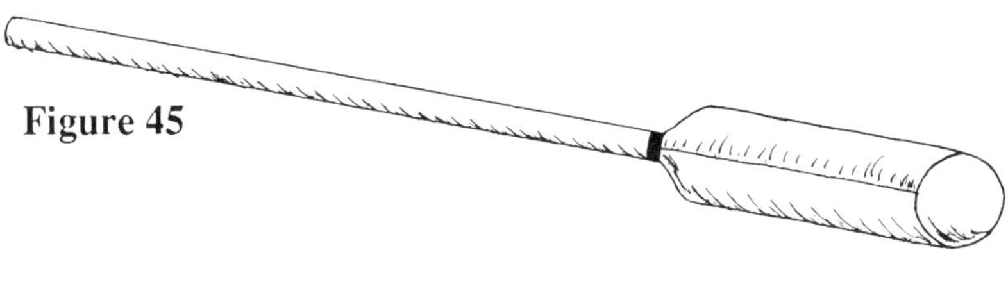

Purchase some soft canvas from a hardware or building supply store. (You may find a better quality of canvas at an upholstery supply store or fabric store.) You'll need two pieces of material, one long and straight and one circular. Sew them together about halfway, as shown in Figure 43, and lay the padded end of the stick inside the material. As you begin to sew the canvas cover closed, as in Figure 44, be sure that the fit is very tight and the pad is going to be firm. If there is any slack or laxity in the cover, add more cotton. If the cover fits sloppily, the cotton under it will begin to shift eventually, and there will be portions of the stick with too little padding, especially at the tip, where padding is most important.

When you have sewn the canvas cover closed (Figure 45), tack the end of it to the stick with upholstery nails and cover the nails with nylon or cloth fiber tape.

## *Use of the Pugil in Practice*

The pugil stick is not a weapon; it is a training instrument and should be used as such. You do not want to take long wild swings at a training partner, and you don't want to have to block them either. Basically, you are only going to be using two strokes: a lunge or thrust and a horizontal sweep.

Figures 46 and 47 illustrate the lunge stroke. Hold the stick as shown in Figure 46, and thrust it forward as shown in Figure 47. Thrusts should be aimed toward the face or abdomen.

Figure 48 is an overhead view of the path of the pugil used in a horizontal sweep. You would extend it forward as in Figure 47, but aim it at the outside of the head and sweep it to strike the side of the head. The same stroke may be thrown at the ribs.

Figure 46

Figure 47

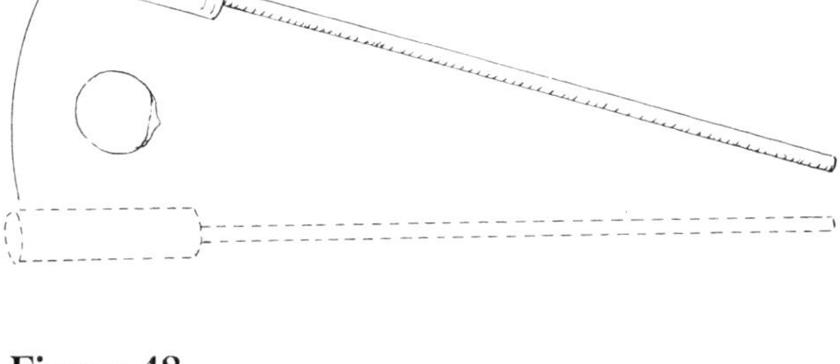

Figure 48

## Safety Projectiles

One of the most interesting methods of training visual perception and conditioning reflexes is with the use of projectiles. Traditionally, projectile weapons such as shuriken and spears were used. However, the same results can be achieved without the element of danger these weapons pose and without the hesitation and apprehension a training assistant might experience when throwing them. As outrageous as it may seem, we're going to make bean bags—twenty to be exact.

Observe Figure 49. Using a soft but strong material, cut forty 8" x 8" squares and draw a 6-1/2" circle in the center of each. Cut out the circles and arrange them into twenty pairs. Sew the two pairs of material back to back, leaving

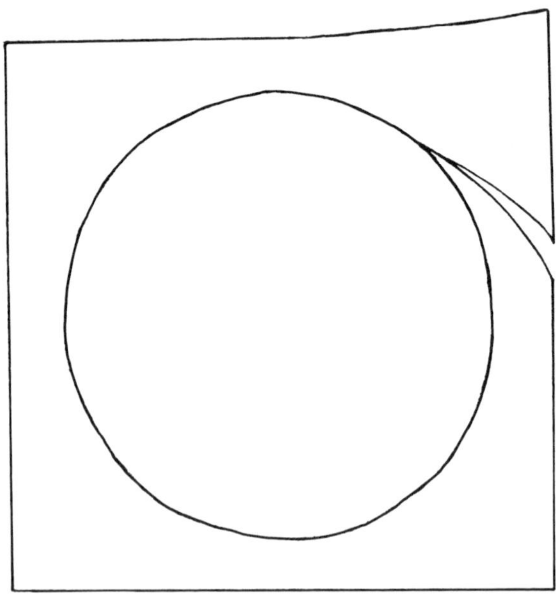

**Figure 49**

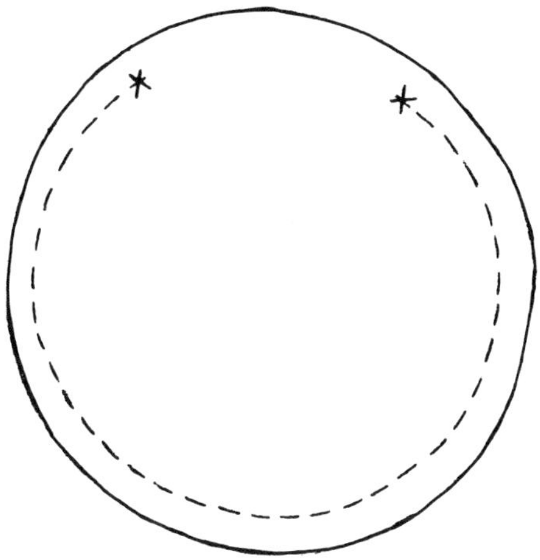

**Figure 50**

an opening at the top as in Figure 50, and turn the material right side out. Fill the bags with dried beans (do not fill beyond the three-quarter mark or your bean bags will have too little give) and sew them closed.

What you now have is twenty projectiles that you can throw at a training partner (or have thrown at you) at full power and speed with minimal risk of injury. The effect of projectile training will be realized quickly in your slipping and blocking ability. The process will be discussed in the following chapter.

## Safety Equipment

There are two final pieces of safety equipment you will need, and though they may also break age-old traditions, they are highly recommended.

The use of a mouthpiece and gloves permits bodily and

facial contact with punches that would be impossible to withstand without protective gear. This allows you to experience the impact of punches—as well as to experience landing your own punches—without the risk of injury to yourself or your training partner. What we are trying to develop with this study is a functional level of skill in a dangerous but necessary art. The process is going to present a myriad of difficulties while demanding many adjustments to new and unfamiliar movements. If nontraditional equipment can reduce the element of danger, it should be used. We are concerned with the long-term goals and effects of our efforts, and such equipment will not harm those goals. On the contrary, it will simplify the effort.

### *Mouthpiece*

A mouthpiece might create some initial discomforts in contact sparring, because it will force you to keep your mouth closed and breath through your nose. However, this will expand your lung capacity more quickly and bring you to your second wind sooner, so the results are well worth the initial discomfort.

The mouthpiece has only one function. It keeps the teeth from being smacked or ground together when a punch strikes the lower half of the face, especially along the jawline. It will not keep you from getting a fat lip, nor will it keep you from losing your teeth from a direct hit from a full-power kick. The proper mouthpiece will, however, alleviate an injury that often occurs in high-speed sparring, wherein a lip gets pushed over the surface of the teeth, resulting in a cut that sometimes requires stitches. It will also alleviate the possibility of teeth being broken or chipped when they are forced together.

Observe Figure 51. This is the type of mouthpiece that

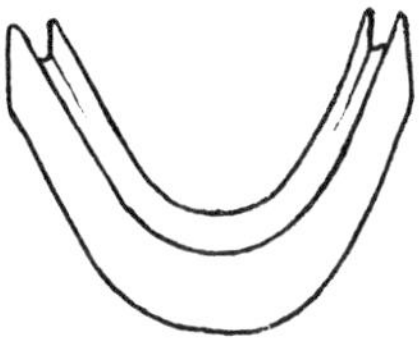

**Figure 51**

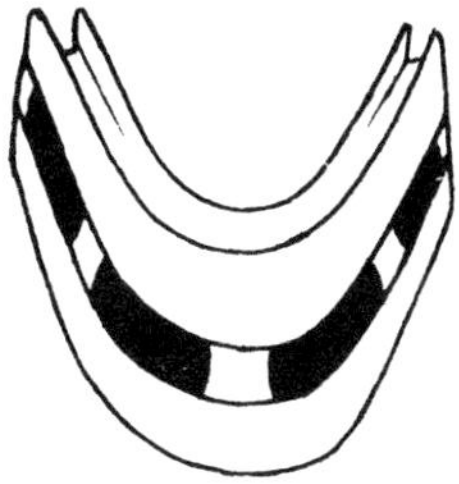

**Figure 52**

fits over either the upper or lower set of teeth. It is not practical for contact sparring. Figure 52 is a double mouth-piece. This is the type you want to use. It provides separate protection for the upper and lower teeth. It has an open area through which you can breath, which serves as a shock absorber as well. For example, it would keep your mouth from being jammed closed if you were hit with a hard uppercut or rising front kick under the chin, and as long as it remained in place, it would make it impossible for a lip to become trapped between the teeth or the mouthpiece itself.

For pugil training, projectile training, and sparring, always wear a mouthpiece. Anytime there is going to be contact to the body using punches, kicks, or training tools, a mouthpiece is the one piece of equipment you can count on to protect your teeth. You will need to rinse it off periodically, but it's worth the effort.

## *Boxing Gloves*

All of the hand strikes used in the Lian Shi system are closed-hand strikes, and all of them are shown with a gloved hand. (A lengthy analysis of striking areas and hand positions can be found in my book, *Iron Hand of the*

*Dragon's Touch*, available from Paladin Press.)

Boxing gloves, like the mouthpiece, will not be a hindrance to training, but rather an invaluable tool that will allow you to train more vigorously without the fear of injury.

You will want to find an eighteen-ounce pair of gloves, and since slip-on gloves tend to slide once they have been used repeatedly, the lace-up gloves shown in Figure 53 are the best value. After you buy the gloves, stop at a fabric store or upholstery supplier and purchase a bag of chipped foam rubber. It will be necessary to make some modifications.

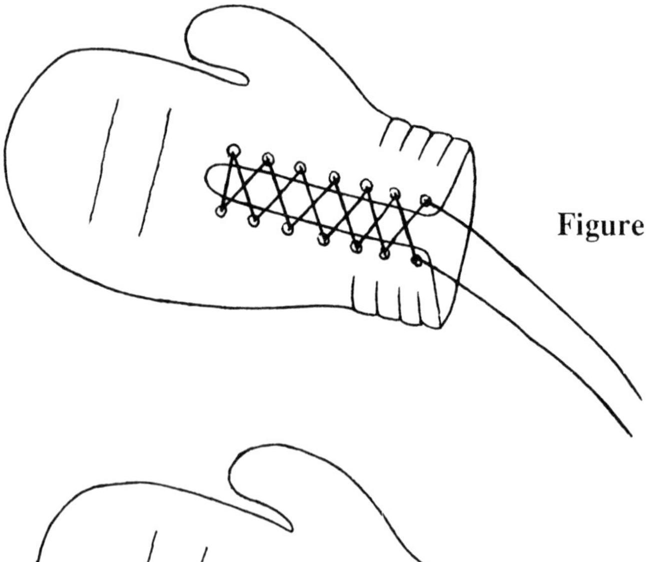

Figure 53

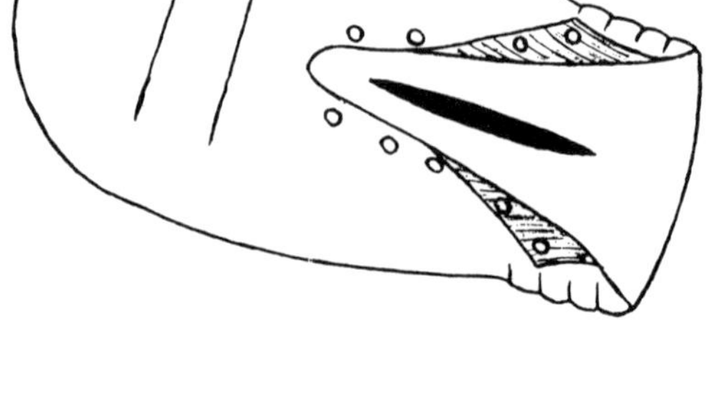

Figure 54

As shown in Figure 54, remove the lacing and make a four-inch incision in the inner lining of each glove. Stuff the gloves with as much of the chipped foam as you can possibly get into them, then sew the incision closed. At first, it will seem as if the gloves are too firm, but after one or two uses they will soften up. Even high-priced gloves will lose their shape after repeated use and develop bare spots on the striking area. The extra foam makes the gloves hold their shape much longer and provides better protection against bone-to-bone contact. An overstuffed glove will not do much to cushion the shock of a punch, but it will almost completely alleviate the possibility of bruising.

You will want to follow some special care procedures for these gloves. First, always remove the strings and prop the gloves open when you have finished using them. And second, always wipe down the surface of the gloves with a disinfectant and use a spray disinfectant on the inside after every use. These simple procedures will allow the gloves to dry properly and keep them free of bacteria.

When you put the gloves on to use them, always put a light coat of petroleum jelly over their surface. Inspect the gloves closely after each use. If a crack develops in the contact area, it is time to get another pair. Using gloves with cracks in the striking surface will almost surely cause skin scrapes.

# 5 RETRAINING THE DEFENSIVE REFLEXES

In the opening chapter, we analyzed the core of defensive capabilities and learned that the natural neurological function known as the reflex arc may be trained to respond instinctively and specifically as a conditioned reflex. The conditioning process is not a theoretical approach to achieving efficiency in the martial arts, but a time-proven process. Each student will develop at his own pace, according to his capacity to grasp the movements, and at a rate proportionate to his dedication and persistence in training.

We are now going to integrate the movements of chapters 2 and 3 with the tools described in chapter 4 and begin the developmental process for the conditioned reflex. We will be referring to these previous chapters repeatedly. Be sure to refer back to the illustrations in those chapters if you are unsure of the discussion. This chapter will focus on defensive training.

## Slips

We will begin with the use of slips against pugil lunges at the face. (Refer to chapter 2, Figures 3 through 12 and chapter 4, Figures 46 through 48.)

### *Right- and Left-Side Parallel Slips*

Assume the practice position illustrated in chapter 2, Figure 3. Position your training partner in front of you with the pugil stick at a range which will allow him to extend it and strike your face without stepping forward. When you are both ready, have your training assistant jab at your face with a lunging stroke. The speed of the jabs should be slow to medium to start, following a repeat pattern of one stroke every five seconds for a duration of two to three minutes.

When you perceive the advance of the pugil, use a right-side or left-side parallel slip to elude it. Do not use a repetitious right-left, right-left pattern to your slips. Doing so will cause your training partner to anticipate your movement and unwittingly begin directing his strokes where he knows you are going to go instead of where you are.

As you begin to feel comfortable with your movements, allow your training partner to increase the speed of the offensive strokes gradually to full capacity.

### *Right- and Left-Side Diagonal Slips*

Once you are able to avoid the higher-speed thrusts, add the right- and left-side diagonal slips to your defensive options, along with right- and left-side sweeping strokes from the pugil. With two new defensive maneuvers and two new offensive strokes from the pugil, your training partner should again start with a slow to medium offensive speed, gradually increasing the speed of the strokes as you feel you are ready for them.

## *Troubleshooting Technique Failure*

There are three very common problems that occur during pugil training.

1) *The pugil is making full contact too often.* You should expect to be hit occasionally, but the contacts should begin decreasing as the practice continues. If this is not the case, concentrate harder on what you are doing and have your training partner slow down the strokes until you are able to avoid them.
2) *The pugil is grazing the head or face.* Either your slips are too shallow or your training partner is following your head unconsciously. Deepen your slips. If the grazing continues, do not move your head when the next stroke comes at you. If the pugil misses you altogether or grazes you without your moving, you will know the strokes are being misdirected. Instruct your training partner to concentrate on striking at your present head position.
3) *Your training partner is having to chase you.* This is a stationary practice. You must learn to hold your position and avoid the strokes without stepping. Concentrate on this mode of practice. You must also be sure to return your head to the starting position after each stroke. Out-of-position slips will be studied at a later stage of training.

## *Forward Slip and the Slip and Weave*

At this point, add the forward slip and the slip and weave movements of chapter 2 to your options (refer to Figures 13 through 20). Again, begin with a slow to medium pace. Be sure you are returning to the starting position each time, and do not decrease the time between the strokes (five-second intervals) at this stage of the process.

## *Step and Slide*

Refer to Figures 21 through 24. The step and slide will be the final addition to the slipping defenses. It should be added in the same manner as the other movements. As with the slip and weave, this addition will be less demanding than the first few techniques. As you become more familiar with defensive movements and how they function, additional techniques will come easier.

The slips should be focused upon for two weeks to two months, according to how quickly you are able to adapt to them. Time spent per session and the number of days per week you train will affect the rate of progress and achievement. When you can avoid 90 percent of the pugil attacks with slips, it will be time to add the formula blocks to your practice. At this time, your training partner should add thrusts to the abdomen to his attack options so that you may utilize the low gate blocks. Spend one week using blocks by themselves, then add the slips. The blocks will present no problem. Your eyes will be familiar with the advance of the pugil and with the concept of defense. The only significant adjustment required is the familiarization of the muscles and bones to the precise movements needed to execute the blocks, and this will come quickly against the strokes of the pugil.

When you have achieved a middling skill level of defense against the pugil, it will be time to enter into a technically higher stage of training to force the development of the reflexes. This is accomplished by having your training partner do his utmost to hit you with the pugil. No more five-second intervals between strokes; no more adjusted speed levels. He is to do his best to hit you, and this practice is to continue until you can avoid 99 percent of his strokes. When you can do this, advance to the projectile stage of training in your defensive system.

## Projectile Training

If you followed the instructions in chapter 4, you will have twenty bean bags to work with. And, if you have adhered to the practice instructions in this chapter, you will have a good understanding of and working ability in slipping and blocking. It is time to put these new skills to work in an advanced training mode.

Begin with your training partner standing fifteen feet away. Assume your blocking practice position (hands up), and have him throw the bean bags at you continuously at five-second intervals to allow you time to return to the starting position. Go through each of the slips and each of the blocks on the first set (twenty bags). Your partner's tosses should be about a three-quarter effort rather than maximum velocity.

If you have been hit with more than two of the twenty throws, repeat the set until you have avoided all but one or two of the bags. When your efficiency level reaches the 18/2 ratio, have the velocity of the throws increased to maximum effort. Maintain the five-second intervals between tosses; this will allow you to return back to the starting position, as well as to focus your concentration on each new throw.

When you have achieved a ratio of 18/2 at maximum output, remove the interval restriction on the tosses. Tell your training partner to try his hardest to hit you with the bags. With the intervals removed, you will now be required to block and slip bags that are coming at you while you are out of position. This will add a new dimension to your defensive training and teach you an important aspect of personal combat: you must be in a state of readiness at all times and remain alert for unexpected attacks.

You will want to train at this level for a month or two while your body and nervous system become familiar with the defensive system. In time, the movements will no longer tax your strength and energy. You will reach the state of "effortless effort." This is the first signal that the reflex arc is beginning to take over your defensive system.

When you have achieved a 100-percent success level in avoiding the projectiles, reduce the distance between yourself and your training partner to ten feet. Have your partner toss the bags with a three-quarter effort at five-second intervals, and work your way back to a maximum effort without intervals.

You will find that the decrease in distance will present a new and demanding challenge, requiring much greater speed in your movements and much quicker perception of the trajectory of the bags. With less time to see the bags, the demand on the reflexes will be much greater, exercising the reflexive process to higher skill and efficiency levels.

This exercise is to be incorporated into your practice permanently. It should become a weekly part of your maintenance training in order to keep your reflexes sharp and in a state of readiness. At this level, you will have developed the specified reflex arc through the conditioning process, and you will have achieved a functional skill that is applicable to self-defense situations.

# 6 OFFENSIVE WEAPONS: UPPER BODY

Before beginning the study of the upper-body offensive weapons, we are going to analyze the base stance a little more closely to note some key posture points.

Look at Figure 55. Notice again that the left hand and shoulder are positioned slightly forward of the right hand and shoulder and that both hands are held at the jawline. The arms are held against the ribs and should be free of tension. The heel of the rear foot is always off the ground, with tension on the gastrocnemius muscle for quick movement. The front foot is planted solidly on the ground for stability. At all times during training and in actual combative situations, the abdominal muscles stay flexed and the shoulders remain relaxed.

## Straight Left Hand (Jab)

We will be spending a greater amount of time studying the straight left hand than we will spend with the other upper body weapons because of the usefulness of the stroke. Traditional boxing matches, kickboxing matches, and streetfights are often won by the use of an effective straight-line punch from the lead hand. As our starting position depicts, the left hand (and shoulder) is the most forward weapon. It is closer to the opponent and must travel a shorter distance to reach him than the other body weapons. Consequently, it will be quicker.

The jab is not only your most effective offensive stroke; it is your most effective defensive stroke. A finely tuned jab can be utilized as a lead-in strike to bring in a hard right hand or a hard forearm stroke. It can also be used as a lead-in to knee strikes, low front kicks, and various other offensive maneuvers. Because of its structural quickness, the jab functions well as a "beat-him-to-the-punch" stroke against a long right hand or a wide hook. By utilizing the step and slide movement illustrated in chapter 2 (Figures 21 through 23) in conjunction with the jab, you can elude even the shorter, straighter punches, while sending out a simultaneous counterpunch. Of all the hand weapons you endeavor to master, spend the most time developing your jab.

## *Stationary Jab*

Observe Figures 55 and 56. To achieve the position in Figure 56, extend the arm forward in a precise straight line from the jaw to the target, rotating the hand to the palm-down position upon contact. Extend the shoulder slightly forward with the flow and direction of the movement. The arm should become rigid upon contact with the target. Do not raise the arm above the ribs as you initiate the motion. The arm should slide off the ribs in a forward direction. All of your movement to achieve the extended position of the stroke should be in one direction, straight forward, with no arc to the hand or arm and no advance motion from the head or shoulder. The shoulder advances just as the arm achieves extension. Any additional movement is unnecessary, wasteful, and serves as a warning to your opponent that you are about to use the hand.

Figure 55

Figure 56

When utilizing the stationary jab, the posture of the stance remains unchanged beyond the extension of the arm and shoulder. There are no steps and no leans. The stationary jab is applied to an opponent who has stepped into your jabbing range. For the stationary jab and all offensive strokes, including kicks, you will want to return to the starting position immediately upon the completion of the stroke.

## *Leaning Jab*

Observe Figures 57 and 58. Initiated from the same starting position as the stationary jab (Figure 55), the leaning jab is an offensive stroke. The dotted line in Figure 58 depicts the stationary jab issued from the same position as the leaning jab. Note first the considerable gain in distance.

**Figure 57**

**Figure 58**

The leaning jab is used to strike an opponent who is either standing or moving just outside your hand range. The hips are brought forward by pushing off from the right foot while extending the right leg. To compensate for the change in posture, the left leg also straightens.

The added reach of the leaning jab allows you to strike an opponent while he is outside your normal hand range without breaking your set position. It is also useful to reach an out-of-range opponent who may be winding up for a long power blow.

## Forward-Step Jab

Issued from the ready position (Figure 55) and combined with a short step (as shown in Figure 59), the

**Figure 59**

forward-step jab, unlike the leaning jab, brings both the stance and the weapon closer to the opponent. Consequently, the stroke will have a firmer base and greater power. The firmer the stance against the negative reaction force, the more total impact the stroke will have (refer to my book, *Iron Hand of the Dragon's Touch*, for more detailed information on negative reaction force).

When the advance step is used, the rear leg will immediately follow in the direction of the momentum, thus resuming the starting position. All of the movements of the arm and shoulder are the same as those of the stationary jab.

**Figure 60**

## *Rear-Step Jab*

The rear-step jab (Figure 60) is used to adjust the distance between you and a charging opponent. A punch thrown from too close a position will have more "push" power than impact power and will lack the snap it takes to deliver an effective blow. To execute the rear-step jab, the movements of the arm and shoulder are the same. The difference is simply that the right foot, rather than the left, will be the first to move.

## Straight Right Hand

Observe Figures 61 and 62. The straight right hand is

Figure 61

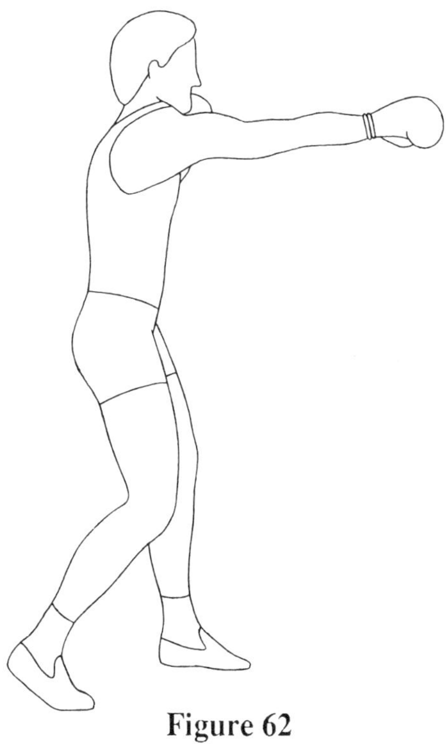

Figure 62

your long-reach power stroke. When the shoulders are rotated into the stroke, the straight right has the same reach that the jab has and will have more power, but because it is being initiated from a greater distance, it will take longer to land on the designated target.

Due to the speed and distance factors, the straight right hand is generally applied as a secondary rather than a lead blow. Depending on the position of the opponent, however, a right-hand lead may be feasible. If the opponent is coming from the right side, then the right hand is closer to him and would have a better chance of landing than the left. Note that in Figure 62, the right hip has been rotated forward along with the leg, and the right shoulder is extended forward into the punch. This has been accomplished without moving the rear foot. The heel is simply brought up higher to allow the weight and power of the hip to flow into the direction of the stroke. Notice that the hand is rotated palm-down at the extension point. In practice and application, the right hand always returns to the point of origin after contact is made.

## Leaning Right Hand

Observe Figure 63. The basic mechanics of the leaning right hand are the same as those of the straight right hand. The leaning right hand requires push-off and extension of the rear leg, straightening of the lead leg, and a deeper advance of the shoulder.

The hips are brought forward and the upper body is tilted forward, resulting in the gain in distance depicted in Figure 64. An increase in total impact power over the straight right hand is indicated, as is the greater reach. The leaning right hand is useful in striking an opponent who is

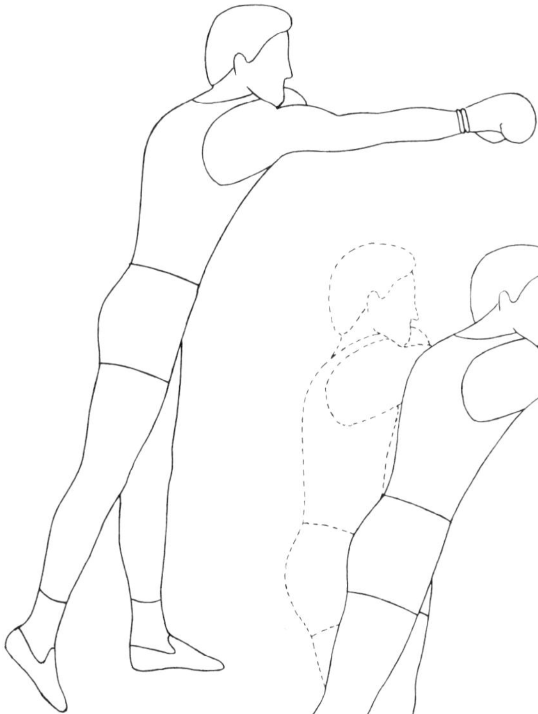

**Figure 63**

**Figure 64**

outside the range of the stationary form of the stroke. It is also useful as a secondary blow when a lead-in jab has been back-stepped or slipped by an opponent. The longer extension of the leaning right hand will allow you to hit the moving opponent who is out of normal range.

## Left Hook

Though it can be effective at a longer range, the left hook is designed primarily for close-contact fighting. The precise angle of the arm and the power source of the punch make the left hook ideal for striking an opponent who is too close for straight-line punches.

**Figure 65**

**Figure 66**

**Figure 67**

Observe Figures 65 through 67. You will begin your motion from the ready position shown in Figure 65. In Figure 66, the left hand is extended to the outside of the designated target. To reach the final position depicted in Figure 67, the entire body, from the knees upward, is twisted to the right to bring the punch to the target, and the arm is held rigid at an angle varying from 90 to 135 degrees (135 degrees being the maximum extension).

Note that in Figure 67 the position of the rear foot has only varied slightly. The major motion of the body is accomplished by rotating the hips and shoulders in a right horizontal direction.

The jab works on the snap/extension principle. The hook works on the principle of drive—to drive the hand with continuous force through the target. The hook is sometimes referred to as a "rib-crusher" punch. The use of the hips and shoulders brings the body weight into play, making the hook a devastatingly powerful blow.

## Uppercut

You will recall our discussion in the opening chapter on the natural instinct to protect the face and eyes. It was stressed that dropping the head and eyes down was dangerous. This will become apparent as we discuss the uppercut. This stroke is designed to be utilized on targets the hand can get beneath. Its trajectory is a rising motion that works very well on an opponent who is leaning forward or has slipped a punch downward and lowered his eyes.

Observe Figures 68 through 70. The uppercut thrown at this height is designed to be used on opponents who tilt their upper bodies forward in the ready position, or who

Figure 68

Figure 69

Figure 70

have thrown a leaning jab or a leaning right hand. In Figure 69, note how the right hand has dropped forward and downward. The hand is turned palm-up at this point. In Figure 70, the stroke is completed. Note that the right shoulder has been brought forward, the rear leg has been brought forward without moving the foot (other than to extend higher on the toes), the hips have moved upward, and the upper half of the body has rotated slightly to the left.

All of these movements have been utilized to bring the maximum force of the body into the punch. The punch drives in an upward direction, and at this level would be aimed at the underside of the chin. The uppercut can also be executed from a squat position.

## Horizontal Forearm

Forearm strokes are designed exclusively for close-in fighting. The strokes are short but extremely powerful. Absorption of expended force into a blow is discussed at length in my book, *Iron Hand of the Dragon's Touch.* In that study, I talked about the fact that joints linking bones together put "give" in the long strokes. There is no give in the forearm stroke. The only joint involved in the movement, the shoulder, is one of the major power sources of that movement. Punches give at the elbow and at the wrist, and due to the extension of the arm, there is additional give at the shoulder. The horizontal forearm stroke has no weaknesses, and so will be a first-choice weapon in clinches and close-in fighting situations. The stroke can also be used with an advancing step or from a block; an example of this will be seen in the chapter on practical application.

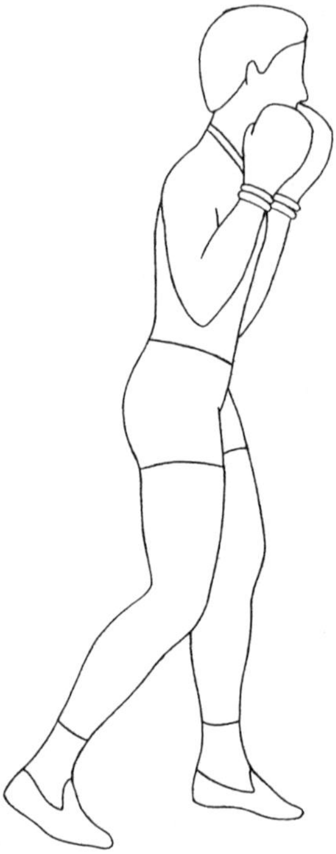

**Figure 71**

**Figure 72**

**Figure 73**

Observe Figures 71 through 73. In Figure 72, the right arm has been raised off the ribs and the hand dropped forward, palm down. In Figure 73, the arm has been powered across the chest with the hand ending up on the left side of the face. The trajectory of this stroke makes it most applicable to striking the jawline or across the sternocliedomastoid region of the neck. The temple is also a good target for this stroke.

The pectoral and anterior deltoid muscles are the powering force behind the horizontal forearm, and you will find the stroke particularly useful in street applications. It is difficult to practice because there is no way to effectively pad the elbow or the forearm to make it safe to strike a training partner, so this stroke will have to be done on training equipment.

## Vertical Forearm

The vertical forearm will take the same form as the uppercut. Both strokes work with a rising trajectory and use the same muscles to power the movement. The only difference is the striking instrument and, of course, the areas of give noted in the discussion of the horizontal forearm.

**Figure 74** **Figure 75** **Figure 76**

The forearm will not raise off the ribs and to the side with the vertical stroke. Since you will be striking in a forward and upward motion, the elbow will leave the side in precisely that fashion—forward and upward. Note that the arm is folded, positioning the hand at the right side of the head. If the left hand were being used, it would be positioned similarly at the left side of the head.

# 7 OFFENSIVE WEAPONS: LOWER BODY

Utilizing the legs as weapons in self-defense gives the student many advantages. Legs are longer than arms. Consequently, a greater reach is achieved. Legs are stronger than the arms; therefore, the potential for impact power is greater. Beyond the obvious, legs are more difficult to block and more difficult to see coming.

Kicking techniques have their limitations, of course. Using kicks from too close a range will rob them of impact power, and the effect will be more of a push than a thrusting snap. A kick thrown so slowly that it is caught in the arms of an opponent can turn the tide of the battle very easily. All things considered, however, kicks are devastatingly powerful and invaluable in self-defense situations, and they should be pursued to the point of perfection.

## Front Kick

The front kick is the most common and most natural of

the kicking movements, the mechanics of which are easily grasped.

The starting position (Figure 77) remains the same, as this is your fighting position. In Figure 78, the right leg is brought forward. You will note that the foot of the kicking leg is only bent back slightly. It is unnecessary and incorrect to wind the kick up by folding it beneath the buttocks. Raise the leg as illustrated.

Figure 79 depicts the extension point. The front kick makes a rising arc and extends into the target by the power of the quadriceps and the forward motion of the leg from its point of origin. The inset illustration depicts an alternate position of the foot when applying the front kick. The position in Figure 79 is called the bridge position; the one shown in the inset illustration is called the ball position. In the ball position, the toes are bent backward and the ball of the foot is used as the striking surface. In the bridge position, the toes remain extended and the bridge of the foot is used as the striking surface. Bridge kicks work well against surfaces that are firm but not hard, including the ribs and other moving bony areas such as the jawline, but you would not want to use the bridge position against the skull, forehead, or the front sides of the limb joints. The ball formation is best suited for the bony targets such as the temple, chin, and sternum.

Since raising the leg to the position illustrated in Figure 78 will require a shift in weight, this position should be practiced repeatedly to familiarize the body with the change in balance. When practicing this kick, follow the sequence of illustrations and then return the kicking foot to the floor by reversing the sequence.

The kick should be practiced with pauses between movements wherein each frame of the sequence of illustra-

Figure 77

Figure 78

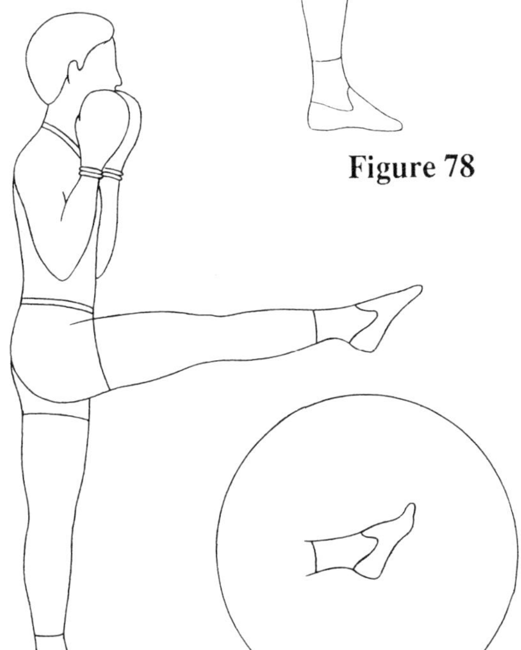

Figure 79

tions is mimicked, and also in a smooth, flowing motion, from origin to extension to origin.

### *High Front Kick*

The only significant difference between the form of the front kick in the high position and the front kick in the low position is the height of the knee at the chamber, or "draw" position.

Observe Figures 80 through 82. In Figure 81, note that the knee is held much higher than in Figure 78, which depicted the front kick at the low- to mid-range height. The leg will extend in line with the height of the thigh. Pointing the knee at the target will ensure that the kick lands on it if the leg is fully extended. Note also that the foot is in the ball position. When the front kick is applied to upper body targets, the foot will have to be held in the ball position. If you use the bridge position, your toes will surely be sprained or broken upon contact with the target. *All high front kicks are to be executed with the foot in the ball position.*

## Roundhouse Kick

In our first two kicks, we began and completed the stroke on a vertical plane. With the roundhouse kick, we will begin with vertical movement but complete the stroke horizontally.

Observe Figures 83 through 85. As always, we are starting from our ready position (Figure 83). The stroke is initiated by shifting the balance forward onto the left leg and raising the knee to the position depicted in Figure 84. To bring the stroke to the impact point shown in Figure 85, the hips are snapped over to the left, allowing the heel of

Figure 80

Figure 81

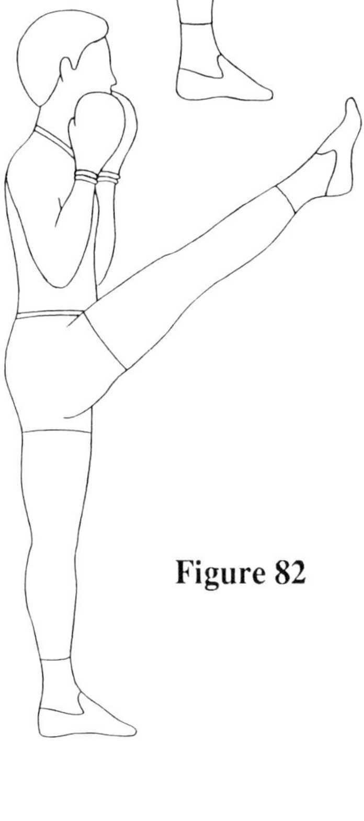

Figure 82

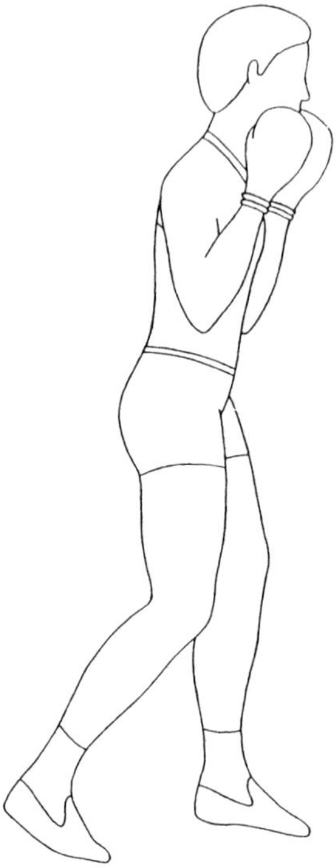

Figure 83

Figure 84

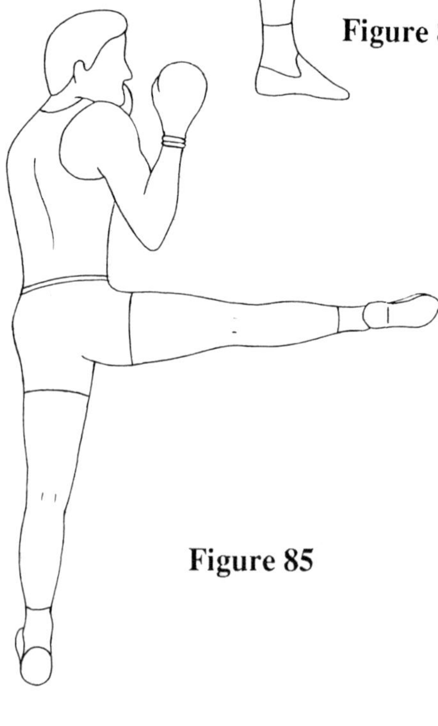

Figure 85

the left leg to rotate counterclockwise. The lower half of the leg is snapped fully open simultaneously, creating a horizontal thrust. Like the hook punch, the roundhouse kick rises on the outside of the target and then turns inward to make contact.

It is crucial to rotate the heel of the standing foot as the kick is snapped. If the heel does not rotate, the hips will

**Figure 86**

**Figure 87**

**Figure 88**

bind the stroke and interrupt the power source, rendering the kick harmless.

Thrown at this level, the roundhouse kick is aimed at the ribs, kidneys, or abdomen, and can be thrown with either leg. When the left leg is used, the movement applies as a lead-in or defensive kick. When the right leg is used, the application is generally a secondary or offensive stroke.

### *High Roundhouse Kick*

The high roundhouse kick utilizes the same mechanics as the low roundhouse kick, the only significant difference being the tilt of the upper body (Figure 88), which is used to counterbalance the height of the leg and the resulting off-centered weight distribution.

## Side Kick

While the side kick is the most difficult kick to master, it is also the most useful and versatile. It is easily applied to an array of anatomical targets, from the shin bone to the forehead, and is completely mobile in a 180-degree radius on both the left and right sides. It can be applied as a long thrust or a short snap, with a high percentage of impact power for either. Just as you spent additional time developing the jab, you should put at least a comparable effort into mastering the side kick.

We are going to study the side kick as applied to an opponent who is directly in front of you, and we will apply it at three different levels. An additional in-depth study of the side kick can be found in my book, *Iron Hand of the Dragon's Touch.*

**Figure 89**

**Figure 90**

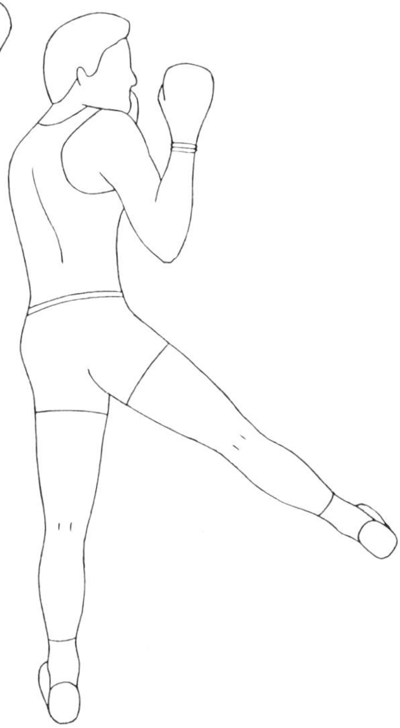

**Figure 91**

## *Side Kick, Low-Range*

Observe Figures 89 through 91. Note that the first two positions are the same as those in the previous kicks. To achieve the extension point depicted in Figure 91, rotate the left heel counterclockwise to the position shown, and extend the leg into the target.

A key to the side kick is the direct line from the hip, through the heel, and into the target. Look at Figure 90. Stand with the right hip against a wall and rotate the left heel until it is pointed toward the wall. At that point, the buttocks should be flush against the wall, the kicking leg still bent. Now extend the leg so that the heel of the kicking foot is riding along the wall. As the kick advances toward the point of extension, the back of the knee joint should be moving synchronously toward the wall. At full extension, the leg should be parallel to the wall.

This study/practice method should teach you that, unlike the front and roundhouse kicks, the side kick does not use the knee as a fulcrum point. As the kicking foot of the front and roundhouse kicks approaches the point of extension, there is an arc in the trajectory of the kick. In the side kick, a direct line is formed from the hip to the target, and the heel rides along this line through impact. In this low-range side kick, the targets are the knees and other pressure points in that area.

## *Side Kick, Mid-Range*

The mid-range side kick (Figures 92 through 94) will follow the same mechanics as the low-range side kick. The targets will change to such pressure points as the substernal notch, heart, solar plexus, and so on, but the form and execution do not change.

**Figure 92**

**Figure 93**

**Figure 94**

### *Side Kick, High-Range*

Observe Figures 95 through 97. Here again, your form will remain unchanged, with one exception. Look at the extension in Figure 97. You will notice the compensation at the upper torso to counterbalance the height of the leg. When kicks are taken to this height, it is necessary to tilt the upper body back slightly to keep the body weight behind the kick. A high kick thrown with the upper body perfectly erect will lack the ability to resist negative reaction force and will lose potential impact

Figure 95

Figure 96

Figure 97

## Rising Knee Strike

The rising knee strike is as simple as Figures 98 and 99 suggest. The leg is driven in an upward vertical plane, with the lower half of the leg remaining at a 90-degree angle to the floor. The rising knee strike is best suited for an opponent who is charging forward to tackle you, grab you around the waist to drive you backwards, or pick you up off your feet to throw you on the floor. Keep the hands in the prescribed position to guard against any wild roundhouse punches that may be thrown at you in the course of the grappling attempt. This strike may also be applied when an opponent has slipped forward and lowered his eyes or when he is bent forward for any other reason. Expect the most from this strike. Like the forearm, the knee has no point of give in its structure. Thrown at the face or head, the knee most often results in a knockout if powered forcefully.

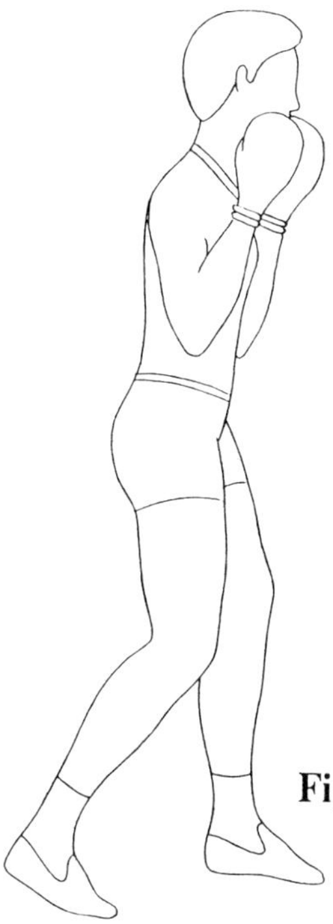

Figure 98

Figure 99

# 8 OFFENSIVE WEAPONS TRAINING

In the last two chapters, we learned a variety of upper and lower body weapons. Just as you had to train to master the defensive movements, you must practice in order to bring the offensive movements to a level of efficiency that will make them of use to you. In training offensive weapons, you will not be as dependent upon the help of a training partner; as a matter of fact, only two additional tools will be required: a heavy bag and a full-length mirror.

## Mirror Training

What a mirror provides to a student is supervision—his own. Initially you are looking for perfection of form. Observe, for example, your straight-line punches to be sure they are actually following a straight line. All of the offensive weapons should be trained according to the guidelines for proper form described in the text. Begin with slow movements, using your own reflection as a target. Run through your set of punches; then run through your kicks.

Observe them for form. You will find most of them to be uncomfortable to perform as described. Your muscles and joints, being unfamiliar with the movement, will tend to follow their own course. The mirror will make you aware of this and allow you to make the necessary adjustments to avoid developing incorrect technique. Slowly add speed and power to your movements, maintaining the correct form.

You will also want to position yourself at an angle to the mirror and observe your movements from another point of view. The angular position will allow you to observe your technique for full extension.

Every offensive weapon has a two-stroke movement—first to extension and then back to chamber, or starting position. When a weapon is used, it must be returned to the chamber position so that it may be reused, as with reloading a gun. When you are able to extend your punches and kicks properly, you must work to achieve the skilled, speedy return of the weapons. When a combination strike is used, such as a jab followed by a right hand, the right hand is extended as the jab is returned. The right hand returns by itself. Separating the movements—waiting for the return of the left hand before extending the right toward its target—would result in a loss of delivery time.

You will want to be cautious in the return of the weapons. If you should fail to return a left hand, for example, and then throw a right, both hands would be out in front of you, leaving no upper body weapons in chamber and available for either punching or blocking. Your rule here is that when throwing combinations, one hand must be returning to chamber while the other is extending toward the target. Never let two hands be fully extended at the same time.

## *Upper Body Practice Sequences*

Observe the following number sequence when practicing your hand strokes with combinations: 1) jab; 2) right hand; 3) left hook; 4) right uppercut; and 5) rear-step jab.

A) 1: jab, return to chamber.
B) 1-2: jab, right hand, return to chamber.
C) 1-2-3: jab, right hand, left hook, return to chamber.
D) 1-2-3-4: jab, right hand, left hook, right uppercut, return to chamber.
E) 1-2-3-4-5: jab, right hand, left hook, right upper cut, rear-step jab, return to chamber.

To train these sequences, begin with A. Snap out the jab as quick and as hard as you can and return it to chamber. Follow A with B—a snappy jab followed by a right hand. Return the right hand to chamber as quickly as possible. When you feel comfortable with the B sequence, go to C. Be sure you are not sacrificing extension for speed. Extend each punch properly. When you are ready, go on to D. One hand should be flowing smoothly behind the other. The E sequence will add a rear-stepping jab to the D sequence, giving you a five-phase training sequence for hand combinations. Concentrate on flow and continuity of movement. What gives combinations their effect is the *continuous* contact of punches, giving the opponent no time to recover from the previous punch.

## *Lower Body Practice Sequences*

Kicks are trained in the mirror following a very similar sequence, but the chamber of a kick is the knee-up position rather than on the floor where the movement originates. Begin with single strokes, both directly into the mirror and at an angle. Concentrate on form and extension. When the individual movements reach the point of comfort, begin the combination training here, too.

Your sequence is as follows: 1) front kick; 2) roundhouse kick; 3) side kick; and 4) rising knee. You will want to mix up the heights of the kicks at an advanced stage, but to begin, run each sequence at one height: one at low-range, one at mid-range, and so forth.

A) 1: front kick, return kicking leg to the floor, and resume ready position.
B) 1-2: front kick, return kicking leg to chamber, roundhouse kick, return kicking leg to floor, and resume ready position.
C) 1-2-3: front kick, return leg to chamber, roundhouse kick, return leg to chamber, side kick, return leg to floor, and resume ready position.
D) 1-2-3-4: front kick, return leg to chamber, roundhouse kick, return leg to chamber, side kick, bring leg all the way down to the floor and bring up the rising knee strike, return leg to floor, and resume ready position.

You will note that there was no mention of which leg to use. These sequences are to be practiced first on the right side exclusively, then on the left. When the techniques begin to flow, begin alternating according to the following specifications: #1 right; #2 left, #3 right, #4 left; and vice versa.

Next, you will want to combine heights on a single-leg, double-stroke kick.

A) front kick high, front kick low.
B) front kick low, front kick high.
C) roundhouse kick high, roundhouse kick low.
D) roundhouse kick low, roundhouse kick high.

E) side kick low and mid-range
F) side kick low and high.
G) side kick mid-range and high.
H) side kick mid-range and low, and so forth.

Combination knees are impractical but should be added as a final stroke in practice.

Finally, you will want to double up kicks while alternating legs: side kick right leg, side kick left leg, and vice versa; roundhouse kick right leg, roundhouse kick left leg, and vice versa; and so on.

Your goal in training these doubles and combinations is to be completely mobile when an opening to land one kick or another appears, and not to be forced to use a certain leg because you are unpracticed in using the opposite leg for the same kick.

## Heavy Bag Training

Once you have reached a high level of skill with the use of a mirror, you will want to integrate heavy bag training into the process. The heavy bag provides two important areas of training for the student. It gives him an object with which to make contact and experience negative impact forces and it gives him an object upon which to unload his full power with the strikes. Making contact with a target when maximum force is applied to the stroke not only allows the student to experience and judge the force of his blows, but develops greater power as well.

You will follow the same sequences used in the mirror training, but the focus will be first on high-impact blows with a goal of increasing power, and then on developing speed using half-power blows.

## *Power Training*

Begin with your punches, throwing each one individually as taught in chapter 6. Put your absolute maximum power into each stroke without breaking the form. After a brief period of throwing singles, begin the sequential training you used in front of the mirror.

You will find that this practice stresses the muscles and joints involved, and this is good. The human body responds to increased demand with increased output. When you repeatedly take the body to its limits, capacity expands correspondingly.

You are concerned not with rapid strokes here, but with full power. Even when throwing combinations, keep your movement flowing from one strike to the next, but focus mainly on maximum impact. Structure your practice of high-impact kicking just as you structured the punching practice.

Design each set to exceed the power output of the previous set: more drive, harder extension and lock out, more effort in both. This is how you build power into anatomical weapons. Power training should be practiced once per week.

## *Speed Training*

Single strokes, sequences, and all the processes applied in mirror training and power training are applied here, but you want to use half power against the target while still throwing the strokes and combinations at full speed.

In training, accuracy is often sacrificed for speed. This weakness will manifest itself at the most critical moment: in an actual self-defense situation. To avoid this, it is essential that you maintain your form and accuracy at a 50-percent power level while pushing to develop speed.

Begin with single strokes, then advance to combinations with both the upper- and lower-body weapons. When you get to the doubles and combinations, work for an ever-increasing amount of speed and a reduction of time between contact. This will condition the nervous system to operate at full speed comfortably, and with each practice session it will take less and less effort to use this speed. Like power training, speed training should be practiced once a week.

# 9 PRACTICAL APPLICATION

It is time to put your studies to work against actual attacks. Have your training partner—wearing gloves and a mouthpiece—throw the following single-stroke attacks at you. Begin at a medium pace, adding speed as you are able to handle it effectively. Your counterstrikes should make contact lightly so as not to injure your partner. You have already developed all of the tools of the art of self-defense; this is nothing more than an applied exercise.

## Series 1: Leaning Speed Jab

Begin in the ready position, as shown in Figure 100. In Figure 101, your opponent is throwing a right-hand lead punch. In Figure 102, you lean forward and snap out your jab. Your arm has traveled inside the stroke of your opponent.

*Commentary*: The speed jab works best when you are set and waiting for the opportunity to use it and your opponent has moved in with his attack from outside your range. You

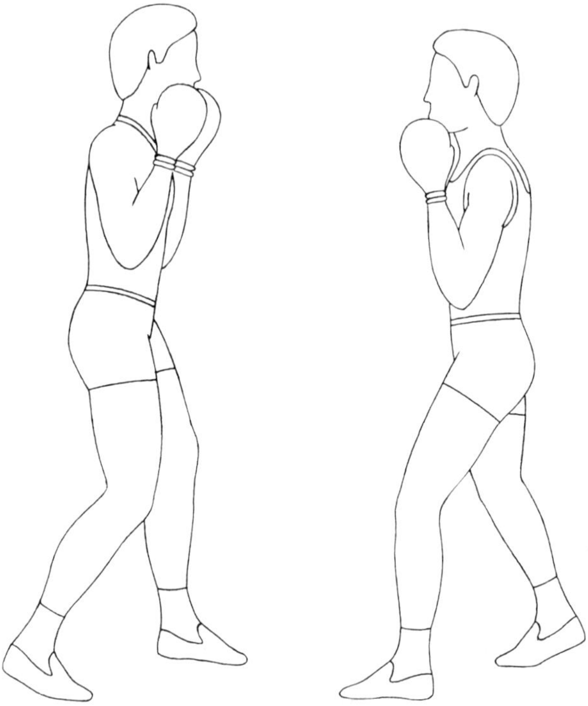

Figure 100

Figure 101

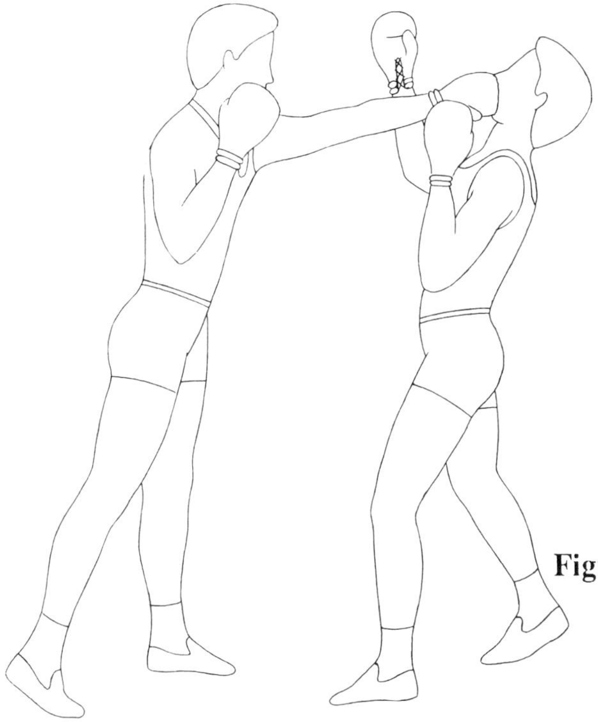

Figure 102

may apply the same technique to an opponent's jab by using the left step-and-slide slip.

*Alternate*: After the jab has landed, retract the left hand while extending the right straight-line punch. Hold your leaning position until the right hand lands, then return to the ready position.

## Series 2: Left Palm Block, Straight Right Hand

Begin in the start position indicated in Figure 103. In Figure 104, your opponent is throwing a right-hand lead punch to the center of your face. Figure 105 depicts a left palm block. As indicated in Figure 106, extend the block to carry your opponent's arm to the outside of your right shoulder. Snap out a right straight-line punch, as shown in Figure 107.

Figure 103

Figure 104

Figure 105

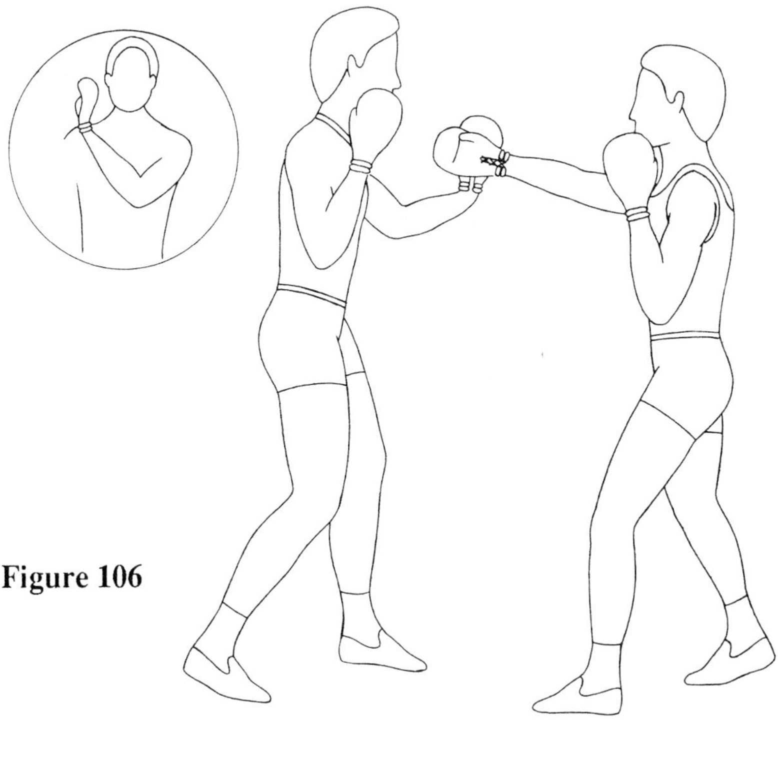

Figure 106

Figure 107

*Commentary*: The counterpunch may be thrown to the heart or solar plexus if the opponent's arm is high and covering the chin.
*Alternate*: Follow through with a right front kick to the groin or a left hook to the head.

## Series 3: Left Palm Block, Right Uppercut

Get into the starting position (Figure 108). Again, your opponent is throwing a right-hand lead punch to the center of your face (Figure 109). In Figure 110, you apply a left palm block, pushing the opponent's hand to your right shoulder as you drop your right hand for an uppercut. Note the position of the arm in Figure 111. The uppercut is thrown under the opponent's arm.

Figure 108

Figure 109

Figure 110

Figure 111

*Alternate*: From the position in Figure 111, a left hook is a perfect secondary punch.

## Series 4: Front Kick

Assume the starting position (Figure 112). In Figure 113, your opponent is throwing a right-hand lead punch, and you have chambered a right front kick. Observe Figure 114. You have snapped out your front kick. Your foot is in the ball position. Your target is the solar plexus or the abdominal muscle group.

*Commentary*: As with the leaning speed jab (Series 1), you have been waiting for the opportunity to use this technique on your opponent.

*Alternate*: A good follow-up to this kick would be to step down close to the opponent and bring up a left rising knee strike.

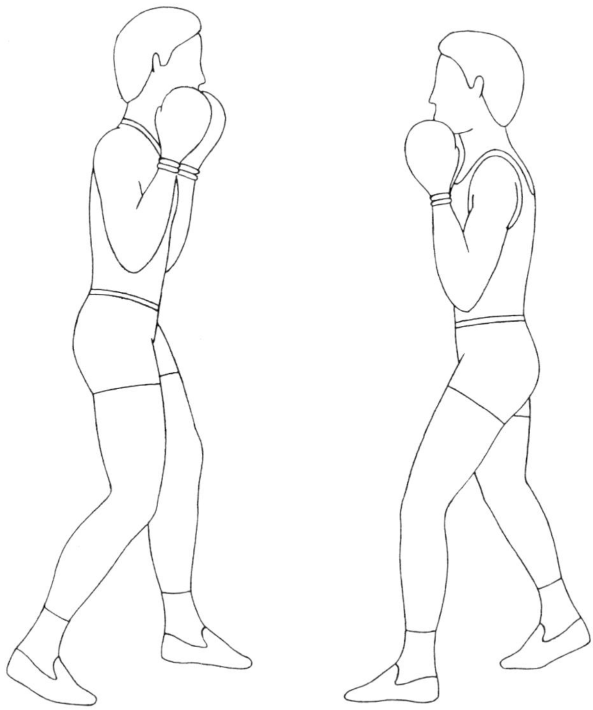

**Figure 112**

Figure 113

Figure 114

## Series 5: High Front Kick

Begin in the ready position, as in Figure 115. In Figure 116, your opponent is throwing a right-hand lead punch, and you have chambered your right leg for a front kick. In Figure 117, you have snapped your front kick out, striking your opponent's chin.

*Commentary*: As noted in chapter 7, the high front kick is always used with the foot in the ball position.

*Alternate*: If the kick lands solidly but the opponent does not go down, rechamber the right leg and shoot out a mid-range side kick to his abdominal region.

**Figure 115**

Figure 116

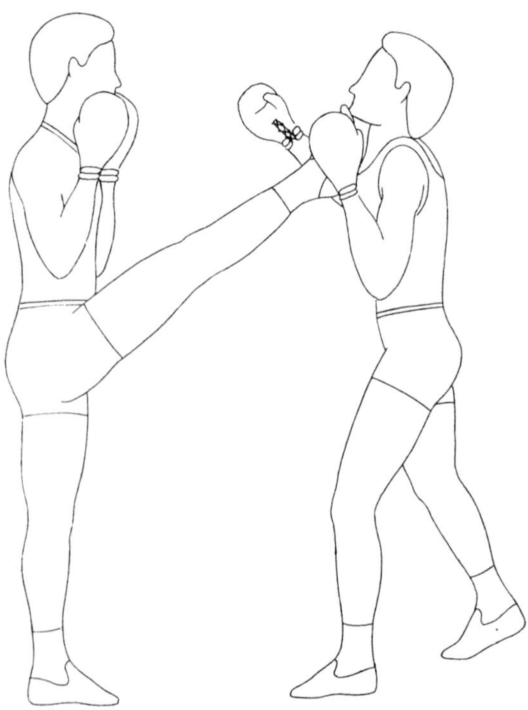

Figure 117

## Series 6: Low Side Kick

Get into the starting position (Figure 118). Observe Figure 119. Your opponent is throwing a right-hand lead punch, and you have chambered the right leg for a kick. In Figure 120, you snap your side kick down into the anterior section of the knee joint.

*Commentary*: When properly powered, a low side kick to the knee will alleviate the need to use a follow-up stroke.

**Figure 118**

Figure 119

Figure 120

## Series 7: Mid-Range Side Kick

Begin in the ready position, as in Figure 121. Your opponent is throwing a right-hand lead punch in Figure 122, and you have chambered your right leg for a kick. Observe Figure 123. You have snapped your side kick out to your opponent's midsection.
*Alternate*: Rechamber the kick and snap out a second side kick to your opponent's knee or face.

**Figure 121**

Figure 122

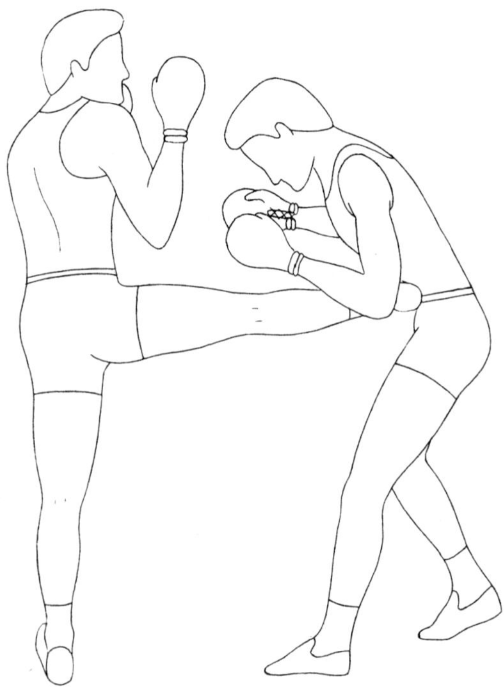

Figure 123

## Series 8: High Side Kick

Assume the starting position (Figure 124). Observe Figure 125. Your opponent is throwing a right-hand lead punch, and you have chambered your right leg for a kick. In Figure 126, you have snapped your side kick out high to your opponent's chin.

*Commentary*: You will find that a side kick landing on an opponent's chin will send him stumbling backwards. If the impact of the kick completely overwhelms his body weight, he will flip backward and fall under your kicking foot.

*Alternate*: If the opponent stumbles backward, set your right foot down ahead of the left instead of chambering the leg, and bring a left roundhouse kick up to his head.

**Figure 124**

Figure 125

Figure 126

## Series 9: Palm Block and Roundhouse Kick

Begin in the ready position (Figure 127). In Figure 128, your opponent is throwing a left jab to the center of your face. Block with a right crossing palm block and chamber the right leg for a kick, as in Figure 129. Push the opponent's hand to the right side of his body and snap out a right roundhouse kick to his ribs, as in Figure 130.

*Commentary*: If your push on the opponent's left hand is strong enough, it may rotate his body to the right, exposing his kidney. A kick to the kidney is more effective than a kick to the ribs.

*Alternate*: A strong follow-up would be to rechamber the leg and throw a low side kick at the knee.

**Figure 127**

Figure 128

Figure 129

Figure 130

## Series 10: Palm Block and High Roundhouse Kick

Assume the starting position (Figure 131). In Figure 132, your opponent is sending out a left jab to the center of your face. Block with a right crossing palm block and chamber the right leg for a kick, as in Figure 133. Push the opponent's hand to the right side of his body and snap out a high roundhouse kick to his head (Figure 134).

*Alternate*: While the opponent's arm is up and out of the way, rechamber the leg and throw a mid-range side kick.

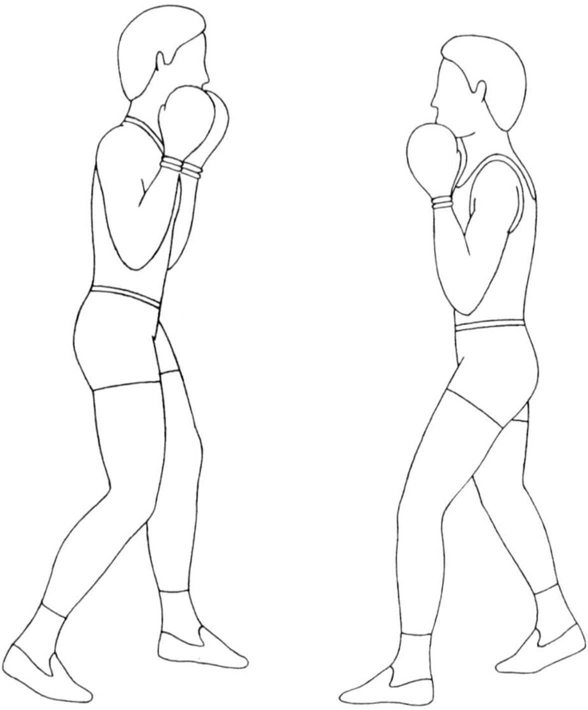

Figure 131

Figure 132

Figure 133

Figure 134

## Sparring

After practicing these basic techniques, you will be ready for sparring, which is the practice rendition of a fight. There are no predetermined movements or limitations. You will want to begin at a moderate speed and intensity, increasing both as you and your training partner are ready. You are not trying to hurt each other, but rather giving each other the advantage of experiencing combat minus the danger of serious injury. Work to help each other grow in skill. A better training partner will mean a more productive practice session. Work your movements as you have learned them. If at any time either of you becomes angry during the session, have the wisdom to stop sparring and work on a noncontact form of training. Heated sparring sessions are of no benefit to anyone, and may very well result in serious injuries. Sparring should be an enjoyable challenge, not a competition.

# EPILOGUE

This text goes a step beyond instructing on movement, and even beyond the methodical skill-gaining process. The format, if followed with dedication and adherence to the instruction, will in time create the state of "second-nature" defensive ability—the development of the specified reflex arc. It is that peerless level of achievement which a student should seek to accomplish in training, and he must settle for nothing less.